· PLAY & LEARN ·
TODDLER ACTIVITIES BOOK

· PLAY & LEARN ·

TODDLER ACTIVITIES BOOK

200+ Fun Activities for Early Learning

ANGELA THAYER

ILLUSTRATIONS BY TYLER PARKER

ROCKRIDGE
PRESS

Illustrations by Tyler Parker/Illozoo
Design by Stacy Wakefield Forte

Photography © Suzanne Clements/Stocksy, p. ii; Meaghan Curry/Stocksy, p. xii; Weekend Images Inc/iStock.com, p. xvi; Pansfun Images/Stocksy, p. 6; Michela Ravasio/Stocksy, p. 54; Lauren Naefe/Stocksy, p. 104; Kristen Curette Hines/Stocksy, p. 156; Tara Romasanta/Stocksy, p. 202; Buzzzzzz/iStock.com, p. 252.

Author photo by Katie Evans Photography

ISBN: Print 978-1-93975-483-7 | eBook 978-1-93975-484-4

TO MY WONDERFUL
HUSBAND AND CHILDREN.
THANK YOU FOR ALWAYS
ENCOURAGING ME
TO DREAM BIG.

CONTENTS

2 CREATE

7

CONTENTS

3 EXPLORE

55

4 PRETEND

105

5 SENSE

157

CONTENTS

6 PLAY

203

INTRODUCTION

LET ME BEGIN with a story about the importance of play. The first time I set up an activity for my toddler, Troy, I created a farm-themed sensory bin complete with dry pinto beans, miniature pumpkins, little buckets, tiny shovels, plastic farm animals, and an assortment of tractors. I was nervous. Would this activity really keep his attention? Would he learn anything? Or would it just create a big mess? As I sat and played with Troy, I saw the wheels turning in his brain. I saw him scooping up the beans with the tractor and filling up the wagon. He was digging and burying the pumpkins. When the beans started spilling out of the tractor, he figured out a way to keep them in their compartment while keeping the tractor in motion. It was a beautiful moment. He was being imaginative and creative and solving problems. The best part of this activity was that Troy was playing and learning at the same time, but didn't know it!

Play is important for toddlers. Mr. Rogers said it perfectly: "Play is often talked about as if it were a relief from serious learning. But for children, play is serious learning. Play is really the work of childhood." Children learn so much through play-based activities. They make connections, solve problems, use creativity, practice language skills, use their imagination, and much more.

The problem with today's society is that our schedules are fast-paced and we have a habit of overusing screens, especially when raising our children. Unfortunately, this results in less time for children to play. Setting aside time for toddlers to play is vital to their development. It's important to a child's physical and mental health, just as getting enough sleep, eating well, and exercising are. The brain develops most rapidly between birth and age five, especially during the first three years of life, which makes the toddler years—generally defined as the time between the ages of one and three—a critical time for learning. I have seen firsthand the benefits of learning through play. With my 17 years of experience working with children and raising three boys, I've observed how these kinds of activities impact their development. Not only are these activities fun for children, they also make memories and build lasting bonds.

The activities in this book are play activities, yet they all have an educational component. The activities are primarily aimed to help your child learn, but they are also hands-on and fun. Each activity in the book will lay out precisely which skills your toddler is working on, and many activities contain multiple learning components. The activities are designed specifically for toddlers and for you to do with your child, not as independent activities.

Children learn so much during the toddler years. Providing time to play will benefit your child cognitively, socially, emotionally, and physically. The days may be long, but the years do fly by. These activities will help you make the most of these wonderful early years.

• SKILLS LEARNED •

hand-eye coordination

shapes

communication

fine motor skills

letters

observation

colors

spatial awareness

counting

vocabulary

language

oral motor development

memory

sensory development

dexterity

123
numbers

social-emotional development

listening

patterns

sorting

gross motor skills

problem solving

1

THE TODDLER YEARS

A CHILD'S BRAIN DEVELOPS rapidly during the toddler years. Toddlers are constantly learning new skills, trying out ideas, mastering new words, and exploring the world around them. In this chapter, I'll share developmental milestones for toddlers and show how they relate to the play-based activities in this book, as well as explain how best to use this book. As you read, keep in mind that these activities are designed to help toddlers grow and develop.

YOUR GROWING CHILD

One of the best parts about learning with your toddler is watching their daily growth. Through new experiences and the routines of daily life, they are practicing motor skills, learning to communicate, discovering their emotions, and developing cognitive skills. Here are the skills that toddlers are developing at each age. Remember that the ages and skills listed are not set in stone and all children are unique in terms of development.

12 TO 18 MONTHS

Emerging toddlers are still learning to master basic skills. During this time, children learn to stand without support, begin to walk, crawl on furniture, squat down to pick something up, crawl up and down the stairs, sit in a chair independently, throw a ball underhand while sitting, carry a large toy without falling, and begin to run. Young toddlers also learn fine motor development skills like clapping their hands together, waving good-bye, scooping objects with tools, and banging objects together. They are also in the beginning stages of speaking. They use one or two words meaningfully, begin to copy words, babble, practice speech sounds, and point to items they want. In the realm of social and emotional development, it's typical for young toddlers to be shy around others who aren't their parents and show fear in some situations. They have favorite items or people. Young toddlers love to repeat sounds or actions to get your attention. Their cognitive development includes exploring new things by shaking, banging, and throwing. They can find hidden objects, copy gestures, start to drink from a cup, and follow simple one-step directions.

18 TO 24 MONTHS

During this stage, toddlers are more stable on their feet. They are able to jump with their feet together, squat down to play, walk up and down the stairs, stand on tiptoes with support, start to use riding toys, kick a ball forward, and throw a ball into a box. Their fine motor development also begins to take shape. Children begin to hold crayons with fingertips and thumb, scribble with writing utensils, turn pages in books, and open containers. Language skills are continuing to develop as well. They can speak and shake their head to indicate yes and no to questions, understand simple commands and questions, name objects around them, and string two words together. This age group likes to pretend and explore, but prefers a parent to be close by. They also show affection to familiar people and may fear strangers. It's very normal for toddlers to have temper tantrums. Cognitively, they know what ordinary objects are by name, point to get the attention of others, and can follow one-step verbal commands without gestures.

24 TO 36 MONTHS

Older toddlers show a lot more stamina and strength. They are able to stand on their tiptoes, jump, ride a tricycle, stand and walk on a balance beam, catch a large ball, and jump over a small stationary object. Two-year-olds are able to manipulate Play-Doh, turn doorknobs, pick up small objects with a pincer grasp, complete a three-piece puzzle, scribble on paper, begin to use scissors, screw lids on containers, string large beads, use a zipper, and correctly use a spoon. Children closer to age three are able to draw a circle, cut a piece of paper in half, trace lines, sort objects, and fasten buttons. For language development, older toddlers experiment with sound levels, speak a sentence with two to four words in it, follow simple directions, point to items in a book, use the past tense and plural words, begin to answer simple questions, speak under-standably, and carry on a conversation. During this age, children learn to make friends and show affection without prompting. They mainly play beside other children, but begin to include other children in play. Toddlers love to copy others, especially adults and older children. When someone is hurt or sad, they may show concern for them.

Occasionally, older toddlers show defiant behavior and often have a wide range of emotions. In cognitive development, older toddlers sort shapes and colors, complete sentences and rhymes in familiar books, play simple make-believe games, use one hand more than the other, follow two-step directions, and name items in a picture book. Children closer to age three are able to work a toy with buttons, levers, and moving parts, play make-believe with dolls and animals, and complete simple puzzles.

HOW TO USE THIS BOOK

Play & Learn Toddler Activities Book contains over 200 activities that are divided into categories: create, explore, pretend, sense, and play. For each activity, you will see a Materials list that consists of items you probably have around the house, such as shaving cream or glue. Prep Time shows you how much time is needed to get the activity ready. Don't worry: A lot of the activities have no extra preparations necessary. Make sure to look for the Messiness rating (on a 1 to 5 scale), since some of the activities are messier than others. I recommend doing the messy ones outdoors or placing a mat on the floor underneath the activity.

Each activity has a Skills Learned section that explains what skill your child is working on, such as memory, motor development, patterns, listening, and more. Many of the art activities practice fine motor skills. For example, working with a paintbrush is great for fine motor development because your child learns to control the brush in the paint, moving their hand and wrist back and forth via small muscle movements. Some activities encourage the use of a vertical surface because bigger arm movements strengthen the upper body. Others emphasize spatial awareness, hand dominance, and engaging the core. Even though these activities target specific skills, toddlers will be too busy to notice!

There are a variety of activities in this book. Try to choose activities that you think your toddler will enjoy and are appropriate for their age and skill level. Some of the activities are for older toddlers who have strong fine motor skills and aren't prone to put items in their mouth. If you know your toddler puts items in their mouth, avoid activities with small parts. Remember, these activities should be completed with adult supervision. Always be within arm's reach when doing them.

There's no need to start at the beginning of the book. Feel free to skip around and do activities that you know your toddler will enjoy. In the index, you'll find activities organized by the name, skills learned, and prep time. This will help you find the ones that are just right for your toddler. Repeat activities to reinforce specific skills or to enjoy them again!

If you're faced with an unmotivated toddler, think about what topics your child enjoys and do an activity based on that topic. For example, if your child is into dinosaurs, find an activity related to them. Then set a short, focused time for the activity. Don't do anything too elaborate; keep the activity simple. If your toddler wants to extend the activity, try adding more to it. Begin with a quick 5- to 10-minute activity and work your way up to 15 or 20 minutes. It may take a while for your child to develop stamina for longer activities.

Lastly, make sure to have fun. These activities are designed to be exciting, enjoyable, and hands-on for your toddler. Make memories, embrace the mess, and have a blast with your toddler!

2

CREATE

REATING WITH TODDLERS is a rich sensory experience for both you and your child. Time spent creating art and music is great for the sense of touch, sight, and sound. Allowing time for toddlers to be creative gives them the opportunity to be artistic, imaginative, and playful. Toddlers are still learning to control a crayon or paintbrush, so be prepared for some messes.

Here are a few tips for "create" time with toddlers:

- Dedicate an art outfit for your child, such as a large T-shirt or an art smock.
- Remember that sometimes washable paints don't completely wash out.
- Use a low table so your child can use their whole body to make art.
- Try to have a washcloth nearby in case there are unexpected messes.
- If you choose a messy activity, complete it outdoors or over a washable tablecloth.
- Encourage creativity, and keep these activities lighthearted and fun!

TOOTHBRUSH PAINTING

MESSINESS

2

PREP TIME

None

ACTIVITY TIME

15 minutes

MATERIALS

Paper

Tape

Washable paints

Paper plate

Old toothbrushes
(flathead toothbrushes work best)

STEPS

1. Tape a piece of paper to the table.

2. Pour paint onto a paper plate.

3. Have your toddler dip a toothbrush into the paint. (Use a different toothbrush for each color.)

4. Paint the piece of paper and create abstract art. Or help your child create letters and numbers by guiding their hand.

5. While creating art, talk about the names of the colors your child uses and even point out what happens when two colors are mixed together.

BLOCK TOWERS

MESSINESS

3

PREP TIME

None

ACTIVITY TIME

20 minutes

MATERIALS

Whipped or shaving cream

Tray

Blocks

STEPS

1. Place a dollop of whipped or shaving cream onto a tray.

2. Dip a block into the whipped cream to add a thin layer of the cream to the bottom of the block.

3. Place the block on the tray. This is your child's starting point for the tower. Continue doing this with the other blocks to build a sculpture or tower.

4. Challenge your toddler to build the tower as tall as they can without it falling.

ABSTRACT WINDOW ART

MESSINESS

3

PREP TIME

5 minutes

ACTIVITY TIME

20 minutes

MATERIALS

Dry erase marker

Washable paint

Paintbrushes

White sheet
(optional)

PREP

Use the marker to draw outlines of objects like flowers, the sun, or people on a window in your house.

STEPS

1. Let your toddler color in the outlines using a paintbrush dipped in washable paint. If your toddler doesn't want to use outlines, don't worry, they can create abstract art. Optional: Hang a white sheet on the other side of the window to see the art better.

2. Be sure to wash the paint off with water when you're done with the activity. Do not let the paint dry on the window.

CREATE A FACE

MESSINESS

2

PREP TIME

None

ACTIVITY TIME

20 minutes

MATERIALS

Paper

Marker

**Plastic page
protector**

Play-Doh

STEPS

1. With your toddler, talk about the parts of their face: eyes, ears, nose, mouth, eyebrows, hair, and so on.

2. Draw a large oval onto a piece of paper using a marker. Place the paper inside of a plastic page protector.

3. Help your child roll Play-Doh into balls and shape the Play-Doh to look like the parts of the face. Talk about where each part goes and add it to the oval.

4. Repeat the activity to make multiple Play-Doh faces.

DRIP DROP WATERCOLORS

MESSINESS

2

PREP TIME

5 minutes

ACTIVITY TIME

15 minutes

MATERIALS

Permanent marker

Old pillowcase or towel

Water

Jars

Food coloring

Dropper or syringe

PREP

Use the marker to draw a large outline of a shape like a star or a heart onto a pillowcase. Create the watercolors by putting an ounce of water into a jar and adding a few drops of food coloring.

STEPS

1. Have your child fill the dropper with the watercolor and squirt it onto the pillowcase.

2. Continue doing this with assorted colors until the entire shape is filled.

3. While creating, talk about the colors and what happens when colors are mixed together.

4. Allow the pillowcase to air-dry.

5. When it is dry, cut around the outline and hang it up for decoration.

POM-POM
BUBBLE STAMP

MESSINESS

4

PREP TIME

5 minutes

ACTIVITY TIME

15 minutes

MATERIALS

Pom-poms

Clothespins

Washable paint

Paper plate

Paper tape

Bubble wrap

PREP

Clip pom-poms onto clothespins. Squirt washable paint onto a paper plate. Tape a piece of bubble wrap to the table.

STEPS

1. Dip pom-poms into the paint and stamp them onto the bubble wrap.

2. See if your toddler can make the bubble wrap pop while stamping.

3. Allow time for the bubble wrap to dry.

   TIP *If you don't have bubble wrap, try this activity using paper instead.*

SPRAY MY NAME

MESSINESS

4

PREP TIME

5 minutes

ACTIVITY TIME

15 minutes

MATERIALS

Permanent marker

**White card
stock paper**

Tape

Cardboard box

Water

Spray bottles

Washable paint

PREP

Write your child's name in large letters on the piece of white card stock paper using the marker. Tape the paper to the bottom of the interior of a cardboard box. Pour a small amount of water (around 1 ounce) into a spray bottle. Squirt 5 to 10 drops of paint into the bottle and shake the bottle to mix it up. Repeat this step with multiple spray bottles and paints to make multiple colors.

STEPS

1. Have your child spray the paint onto the piece of paper. Help them pull the trigger on the bottle if their hands are not strong enough.

2. Talk about the letters in your toddler's name as they spray them.

3. Once the paper is covered in paint, let it air-dry.

STUCK TO THE WALL

MESSINESS

2

PREP TIME

5 minutes

ACTIVITY TIME

20 minutes

MATERIALS

Scissors

Contact paper

Masking tape

Art items:
cut-up tissue paper,
pieces of colored
paper, pom-poms,
googly eyes, foam
shapes, and other
lightweight items
that won't fall off the
contact paper

Muffin tin

PREP

Cut out a large piece of contact paper and tape it to the wall using masking tape. Make sure the sticky side of the contact paper is facing out and place it at the height of your toddler. Put art items in a muffin tin and set it next to the sticky wall.

STEPS

1. Invite your toddler to create art using the various items. Simply place the items onto the sticky part of the contact paper to make a collage.

2. Experiment with which items stick to the wall and which ones are too heavy to stick.

3. Challenge your toddler to create a face or make letters with the art items.

CAUTION *Keep your child away from the scissors.*

TIP *Masking tape can remove paint from walls and painted wooden surfaces. Substitute painter's tape or drafting tape (available in art stores) where appropriate.*

ICE CUBE SCULPTURE

MESSINESS

2

PREP TIME

None

ACTIVITY TIME

20 minutes

MATERIALS

Large bin

50 to 100 ice cubes

Washable paint

Paintbrushes

STEPS

1. Pour the ice cubes into a bin.

2. Use paintbrushes to paint the ice cubes.

3. Observe how the ice begins to melt, which changes how the ice cubes look. Note that when the ice cubes melt, they start sticking to each other and begin to create a sculpture.

BROOM PAINTING

MESSINESS

4

PREP TIME

5 minutes

ACTIVITY TIME

20 minutes

MATERIALS

Masking tape

Paper

Washable paint

Plastic bins

**Small broom,
preferably child-size**

PREP

Tape large pieces of paper to an outdoor wall to create a paper mural. Pour paint into several plastic bins.

STEPS

1. Dip the broom into the paint and spread it onto the wall.

2. Use large arm motions to paint the whole picture.

TIP *If your toddler is young or cannot control a small broom, try using a smaller brush, like a scrub brush.*

TOWER CHALLENGE

MESSINESS

2

PREP TIME

None

ACTIVITY TIME

20 minutes

MATERIALS

Play-Doh

Caps from food packaging

Straws, cut in pieces
(optional)

STEPS

1. Stick small pieces of Play-Doh between the caps to stack them into a tower. Make a pattern using different colored caps.

2. Challenge your toddler to build as high as they can!

3. Try adding in cut-up pieces of drinking straws to make the tower even taller.

SMOOTH AS SILK PUFFY PAINT

MESSINESS
3

PREP TIME
10 minutes

ACTIVITY TIME
20 minutes

MATERIALS
Bowl

1½ cups shaving cream

¼ cup flour

½ cup white glue

Food coloring

Small plastic zip-top bags
(or squeeze bottles)

Scissors

Paper

PREP

In a bowl, pour the shaving cream, flour, white glue, and a few drops of food coloring. Mix thoroughly before adding the mixture to a small plastic bag. Press all the air bubbles out and then seal the bag. Snip a small section of one corner using scissors. Repeat the recipe with other colors.

STEPS

1. Squeeze the puffy paint onto the piece of paper to make designs.

2. Be creative and make abstract art, or try writing numbers and letters.

3. Let the paint dry for at least an hour.

HOMEMADE PUZZLE

MESSINESS
4

PREP TIME
None

ACTIVITY TIME
30 minutes

MATERIALS
10 wide craft sticks

Tape

Stickers

Mod Podge

Paintbrush

Utility knife

CAUTION *Keep your child away from the utility knife.*

STEPS

1. Place 10 craft sticks side by side and use 2 long pieces of tape to stick them together. Flip the sticks over so the tape side is on the bottom.

2. Have your toddler place stickers all over the sticks, making sure each stick has part of a sticker on it.

3. Use a paintbrush to spread Mod Podge onto the sticks, covering the stickers.

4. Allow it to air-dry. When it is dry, remove the tape.

5. Carefully use a utility knife to cut the sticks apart.

6. At the bottom of each stick, write the numbers 1 through 10.

7. Have your toddler practice putting the puzzle together.

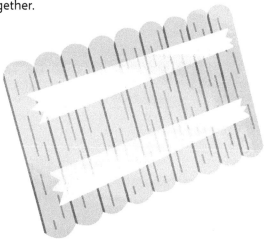

BUNCH PAINTING

MESSINESS

3

PREP TIME

None

ACTIVITY TIME

15 minutes

MATERIALS

20 Q-tips
Rubber bands
Washable paint
Paper

STEPS

1. Gather the Q-tips together and tie them with a rubber band. Dip the Q-tip bunch into paint and stamp them onto the piece of paper.

2. Make color patterns and move the Q-tip bunch across the paper in a line to see what design it makes.

PUFFY CLOUD PICTURE

MESSINESS

2

PREP TIME

None

ACTIVITY TIME

20 minutes

MATERIALS

Paper

Markers

Crayons

Cotton balls

White glue

STEPS

1. Ask your toddler to draw a blue sky on the piece of paper using markers or crayons. Fill the whole paper with blue.

2. Pull cotton balls apart so they are in stretched-out pieces.

3. With a marker, draw several outlines of clouds on your toddler's sky drawing.

4. Have your child dab dots of white glue inside the cloud outlines.

5. Press the cotton ball pieces onto the glue to make puffy clouds.

VEGGIE ART

MESSINESS

3

PREP TIME

5 minutes

ACTIVITY TIME

20 minutes

MATERIALS

Knife

Vegetables like celery, bell peppers, carrots, or cucumbers

Small craft sticks

Washable paint

Paper plate

Paper

PREP

Cut vegetables in halves or pieces. Stick a craft stick through each one so your child can hold the stick and stamp with them easily. Pour paint onto a paper plate.

STEPS

1. Have your toddler place the vegetable stamp into the paint. Try not to get too much paint on it.

2. Stamp the vegetable onto the paper to create a print; practice making patterns.

CAUTION *Keep your child away from the knife.*

MIXED-UP COLORS

MESSINESS

1

PREP TIME

5 minutes

ACTIVITY TIME

10 minutes

MATERIALS

1 cup shaving cream

2 small bowls

**Food coloring in
2 primary colors**

Spoons

**Gallon-size plastic
zip-top bag**

Tape

PREP

Add ½ cup shaving cream to a small bowl and mix in a few drops of food coloring. Repeat this to make two primary colors. Scoop up the shaving cream from each bowl and place it inside the bag. Try to put the colors on opposite sides of the bag. Release the air from the bag and seal it shut. Tape the bag to a table or window.

STEPS

1. Your toddler should use their fingers to squish the shaving cream around and mix the two colors.

2. Observe how the two primary colors mix together to make another color.

3. Swirl the shaving cream around to create designs, shapes, letters, and numbers.

4. Discuss how the shaving cream feels (for example, light and fluffy). If it is taped to a window, it may feel cold.

MIRROR PAINTING

MESSINESS

5

PREP TIME

None

ACTIVITY TIME

20 minutes

MATERIALS

Mirror
Finger paint
Paintbrush
Washcloth

STEPS

1. Take a mirror outdoors and place it on the ground. Set up the finger paints next to the mirror.

2. Let your child use the paintbrush to paint on the mirror. Your toddler can also dip their fingers in the paint if they want to finger paint.

3. Talk about the reflections they see, such as themselves and nature.

4. Encourage your child to create a self-portrait.

HOMEMADE GUITAR

MESSINESS

1

PREP TIME

10 minutes

ACTIVITY TIME

15 minutes

MATERIALS

Rubber bands

Scissors

Empty tissue box

Tape

Styrofoam block

Hot glue gun

Tissue paper

Construction paper

Stickers

CAUTION *Keep your child away from the scissors and hot glue gun.*

PREP

Before the activity, create the homemade guitar. If your child is older, they can help create the guitar with you.

1. Cut five rubber bands so that they lay straight.

2. Stretch the rubber bands over the hole of the tissue box and tape them on the sides. Leave 1 inch of space in between each rubber band. Make sure the tape is very secure.

3. Use a hot glue gun to attach a Styrofoam block to the top of the tissue box.

STEPS

1. Let your child decorate the box with tissue paper, construction paper, and stickers.

2. Have your toddler strum the rubber bands with their fingers to create music.

3. Discuss the different sounds each rubber band makes alone and when strummed together.

CD SUN CATCHER

MESSINESS

2

PREP TIME

None

ACTIVITY TIME

30 minutes

MATERIALS

CD

Items for decorating, like puffy paint, glue, glitter, stickers, and sequins

String

STEPS

1. Let your toddler decorate an old CD on the nonreflective side with whatever they like.

2. Allow time for the CD to dry.

3. Once it's dry, thread string through the hole and tie it to make a loop.

4. Hang it outside on a tree and discuss how it looks when the sun shines on it.

FOIL STAMPING ART

MESSINESS

4

PREP TIME

None

ACTIVITY TIME

15 minutes

MATERIALS

**3 colors of
washable paint**

Paper plates

Aluminum foil

Paper

Marker
(optional)

STEPS

1. Pour paint onto paper plates.

2. Tear off a section of aluminum foil and have your toddler crumple it up in a ball. Repeat to create 3 foil balls.

3. Dip the foil balls into the paint, and stamp them onto the paper to create prints.

4. For a focused activity, draw a simple outline of a flower or tree onto the piece of paper. Then have your toddler stamp colors onto it to fill in the outlines.

MUD TRACKS

MESSINESS

4

PREP TIME

5 minutes

ACTIVITY TIME

20 minutes

MATERIALS

Mud

**Plastic bin,
1 to 2 inches deep**

Dish soap

Water

**Play vehicles like
tractors, cars, or trucks**

Easel paper
(or smaller pieces of paper
taped together)

PREP

Create mud paint by first gathering mud into a bin. Stir in a few drops of dish soap to help the mud spread around more easily. Add a little bit of water to thin out the mud.

STEPS

1. Dip the vehicles into the mud paint and roll it across the paper.

2. Roll the vehicles back and forth and observe the tire marks.

3. Discuss the lines and tracks you see on the paper.

RING NECKLACE

MESSINESS

2

PREP TIME

None

ACTIVITY TIME

20 minutes

MATERIALS

2 toilet paper rolls

Markers or paint

Scissors

Yarn

STEPS

1. Ask your toddler to decorate two toilet paper rolls with markers or paint. Hold the rolls in place for your child if it moves around too much.

2. Allow the rolls to dry, then cut them into 1-inch pieces.

3. Have your toddler string the rings onto a piece of yarn.

4. Tie the yarn together to create a necklace.

CAUTION *Keep your child away from the scissors.*

BUBBLE WRAP ART

MESSINESS

3

PREP TIME

5 minutes

ACTIVITY TIME

20 minutes

MATERIALS

Shaving cream

Bowls

Food coloring

Craft stick

Bubble wrap

Scissors

Gallon-size zip-top plastic bag

Card stock paper

Toy hammer

Scraper or paper towel

PREP

Place a dollop of shaving cream into a bowl. Add a few drops of food coloring and stir with a craft stick. Make 2 or 3 colors in individual bowls. Older toddlers can help with this. Cut bubble wrap to fit inside the plastic bag.

STEPS

1. Spread the various colored shaving cream onto the bubble wrap piece one at a time. Place a piece of paper on top of the shaving cream bubble wrap. Then place it all into a plastic bag.

2. Seal the bag and have your toddler hit the bag with the toy hammer.

3. Take the contents out of the bag. Lift off the bubble wrap and discard.

4. Use a scraper or paper towel to wipe away the remaining shaving cream.

5. Notice how the colors and some circles from the bubble wrap remained on the paper. Discuss how primary colors mixed together to create another color.

CAUTION *Keep your child away from the scissors.*

° SKILLS LEARNED °

COLORFUL PINECONE

MESSINESS

2

PREP TIME

None

ACTIVITY TIME

20 minutes

MATERIALS

White glue

Large pinecone

Tiny pom-poms

Ribbon
(optional)

Hot glue gun
(optional)

STEPS

1. Have your child dab glue all over the pinecone, especially in between the scales. Place small pom-poms on the glue dabs.

2. If you want to hang it up, tie a piece of ribbon and hot-glue it to the bottom of the pinecone.

CAUTION *Keep your child away from the hot glue gun, if using.*

CHALK PAINTING

MESSINESS
1

PREP TIME
None

ACTIVITY TIME
15 minutes

MATERIALS
Bowl

Water

Sidewalk chalk

Construction paper

STEPS

1. Fill the bowl with water. Have your toddler dip a piece of sidewalk chalk into the water.

2. Next, have your child draw on the paper with the wet piece of chalk. If the chalk gets dry, dip it back into the bowl of water.

3. Let the picture dry and watch how the design changes!

STICKER SHAPES

MESSINESS

2

PREP TIME

5 minutes

ACTIVITY TIME

20 minutes

MATERIALS

Easel paper
(or smaller pieces of paper
taped together)

Painter's tape

Marker

Large stickers

PREP

Tape the easel paper to a wall with painter's tape. Draw large shapes on the paper, such as a square, circle, and triangle, with the marker.

STEPS

1. Help your child peel the stickers off their backing.

2. Have your child place stickers on the outlined shapes. Try to fill the whole outlined shape with stickers.

NAME ART

MESSINESS

4

PREP TIME

5 minutes

ACTIVITY TIME

**1 hour, including
drying time**

MATERIALS

Masking tape

**Canvas or
card stock paper**

Washable paint

Paper plate

Dish brush

PREP

Using tape, spell out your child's name on the canvas.
Make sure the tape is very secure. Pour paint onto a
paper plate.

STEPS

1. Have your toddler dip the dish brush into the paint
   and stamp it all around the canvas. Make sure they
   stamp on the tape.

2. Allow time for the painting to dry. Once the paint is
   dry, lift off the tape to reveal your child's name.

CHUNKY PASTA NECKLACE

MESSINESS

2

PREP TIME

None

ACTIVITY TIME

20 minutes

MATERIALS

Ziti pasta

Empty plastic jar

Paint

Tray

Wax paper

Yarn

STEPS

1. Have your child put 5 to 10 pieces of pasta in the empty jar. Squirt some paint into the jar and screw the lid on.

2. Shake the jar until all the pieces are covered with paint.

3. Empty the contents onto a tray lined with wax paper.

4. Repeat the steps with different colors.

5. After the pasta is dry, string the pieces onto a piece of yarn to make a necklace.

SNOW PAINT

MESSINESS

2

PREP TIME

5 minutes

ACTIVITY TIME

20 minutes

MATERIALS

Snow, or ice cubes if you don't have access to snow

Plastic bin

½ cup cornstarch

½ cup water

Bowl

Food coloring

Muffin tin

Paintbrush

Dropper

PREP

Gather snow and put it into a bin. Mix cornstarch with water in a bowl. Add in a few drops of food coloring. Pour the liquid into several compartments of a muffin tin. Repeat the recipe to make more colors.

STEPS

1. Let your toddler dip a paintbrush into the paint and paint the snow.

2. To practice fine motor skills, have your toddler use a dropper to squeeze the liquid onto the snow.

3. Invite your child to use their hands to feel the texture and temperature of the snow.

4. Clean up by disposing of the snow and paint outdoors or in the trash. Do not pour the paint down the drain because the cornstarch could clog it.

PAINT CUBES

MESSINESS

3

PREP TIME

1 hour

ACTIVITY TIME

20 minutes

MATERIALS

Washable paint
Ice cube tray
Wooden craft sticks
Paper

PREP

Pour washable paint into sections of an ice cube tray. Place a craft stick into the paint and lay the stick off to the side of the tray. Place it in the freezer. Once it's frozen, the paint will be a solid cube with a craft stick stuck inside. When you're ready to paint, pull the ice cube tray out of the freezer and let it thaw for 5 to 10 minutes.

STEPS

1. Hold on to the craft sticks and create designs on the paper.

2. Try mixing two colors together and see what color they make. Talk about the different colors on the paper.

3. When the paint begins to melt, the stick will become loose. If you want to reuse the paint cubes, just place them back into the ice cube container and put it back into the freezer.

BUTTERFLY ART

MESSINESS

3

PREP TIME

5 minutes

ACTIVITY TIME

10 minutes

MATERIALS

Cardstock paper

Marker

Scissors

Paint

Paintbrush

Glue

Googly eyes

PREP

Draw the outline of a butterfly onto cardstock paper. Cut it out and fold the butterfly in half.

STEPS

1. Have your toddler paint one wing of the butterfly. Make sure there is plenty of paint on that side.

2. Unfold the other wing and press it onto the painted side.

3. Open the wings; the paint will transfer to the other side and look symmetrical.

4. Add some googly eyes and draw a mouth on the butterfly's head.

CAUTION *Keep your child away from the scissors.*

SWAT THE PAPER

MESSINESS

5

PREP TIME

5 minutes

ACTIVITY TIME

20 minutes

MATERIALS

Tape

Easel paper
(or smaller pieces of paper taped together)

Marker

Paint

Paper plates

Fly swatter

PREP

Tape a large piece of paper to an outdoor wall. Write numbers around the paper using a marker. Pour paint onto paper plates.

STEPS

1. Gently dip a fly swatter into paint.

2. Shout out a number and have your toddler find the number and slap it with the fly swatter. Continue playing the game until all the numbers have been said.

3. To create more art, continue slapping the paper with the fly swatter and paint. Observe how new colors are made when two or more colors overlap.

TIP *Have a dedicated, brand-new fly swatter for playtime—don't use one you normally swat flies with!*

salt Dough Hearts

Valentine's Day is a great time to celebrate love with friends and family. Create these salt dough hearts as a keepsake for your toddler or to give as a gift to a loved one. The directions are simple, so be sure to have your toddler help make the dough and decorate the hearts.

MESSINESS

3

PREP TIME

None

ACTIVITY TIME

1 hour, including baking time

MATERIALS

2 cups flour

1 cup salt

Bowl

Spoon

¾ cup water

Cutting board

Rolling pin

Heart-shaped cookie cutter

Cookie sheet

Parchment paper

Paint (optional)

Sequins (optional)

Glue (optional)

STEPS

1. Preheat the oven to 350°F.

2. Mix the flour and salt together in the bowl using the spoon. Slowly stir in water. If the mixture is too dry, add 1 tablespoon more of water.

3. Knead the dough on a cutting board sprinkled with flour.

4. Flatten the dough with a rolling pin.

5. Use the cookie cutter to create hearts.

6. Lay the hearts on a cookie sheet lined with parchment paper.

7. Place the cookie sheet in the oven for 20 minutes. You may need to adjust the baking time based on the thickness of the hearts.

8. After the hearts are solid, take the sheet out of the oven. Cool them for about 20 minutes.

9. Paint the hearts or glue on sequins.

CAUTION *Keep your child away from the oven.*

POLKA DOT PAPER

MESSINESS

5

PREP TIME

5 minutes

ACTIVITY TIME

10 minutes

MATERIALS

Masking tape

Roll of easel paper

Paper plates

Washable paint

**Small hand roller
or rolling pin**

Bubble wrap

PREP

Tape a long piece of paper to the floor or table. Pour paint into paper plates. Cut a piece of bubble wrap and tape it to the roller with the bubble side facing out.

STEPS

1. Dip the roller in the paint to get a small amount of paint on it.

2. Roll it on the piece of paper.

3. Mix up the colors to make colorful polka dots on the paper.

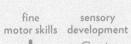
COTTON BALL NECKLACE

MESSINESS

2

PREP TIME

5 minutes

ACTIVITY TIME

1 hour, including drying time

MATERIALS

3 or 4 jars

Water

Food coloring

Paint brushes

Cotton balls

Paper plate

Sewing needle with thread

PREP

Fill each jar with two tablespoons of water. Add a few drops of food coloring to each jar.

STEPS

1. Have your toddler paint the cotton balls. Make sure they are fully covered with color. Allow time for them to dry on a paper plate.

2. Once they are dry, take a threaded needle and string them together.

3. Tie the ends of the thread together and wear it as a necklace.

CAUTION *Keep the needle away from your child if they are not coordinated enough to use it yet.*

FEET PAINTING

MESSINESS

5

PREP TIME

5 minutes

ACTIVITY TIME

15 minutes

MATERIALS

Washable paint

3 or more plastic bins

Roll of craft paper

Heavy objects to weigh ends of paper down

Bucket full of water

Towel

PREP

Pour the paint into at least 3 plastic bins, with one color per bin. Lay out a long piece of paper and weigh each end down with a heavy object. Place the bins on top of the paper, leaving space in between each color. Place a water bucket and towel at the end of the line of bins.

STEPS

1. Dip your child's feet into the first paint bin. Let them walk along the paper and then dip their feet in the next color. (No need to rinse off the previous paint color.) Continue this pattern until your toddler reaches the end.

2. Have your child step into the water bucket and help rinse their feet. Dry their feet off with a towel.

3. Repeat the activity to keep making footprint art and exploring the sense of touch.

NATURE PAINTBRUSHES

MESSINESS

3

PREP TIME

None

ACTIVITY TIME

30 minutes

MATERIALS

Objects from nature

Rubber bands

Washable paint

Cups

Paper

STEPS

1. Go outside with your child and find items to make nature paintbrushes with, such as medium-size sticks, leaves, small flowers, feathers, and various plants.

2. Wrap a rubber band around a stick. Slide one item from the nature collection into the rubber band.

3. Squirt paint into a cup and have your toddler dip the nature paintbrush into the paint and sweep it across the paper.

4. Observe the different strokes each nature paintbrush makes.

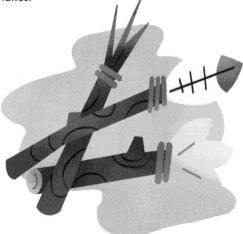

TISSUE PAPER LANTERN

MESSINESS

3

PREP TIME

5 minutes

ACTIVITY TIME

20 minutes

MATERIALS

Scissors

Tissue paper

Paintbrush

Glass jar

Clear glue

Electric candle

PREP

Cut the tissue paper into squares.

STEPS

1. Have your toddler paint the outside of a glass jar with clear glue.

2. Stick the tissue paper pieces onto the glue, making sure all the pieces lie flat.

3. Once the jar is covered, paint a clear coat of glue over the whole jar.

4. Allow several hours for the jar to dry.

5. Once it's dry, place an electric candle inside the jar.

6. Discover what the lantern looks like in a dark room!

CAUTION *Keep your child away from the scissors.*

Thanksgiving Handprint Craft

MESSINESS

2

PREP TIME

None

ACTIVITY TIME

15 minutes

MATERIALS

Card stock paper

Crayons or markers

Googly eyes

Glue

Scissors

Make an adorable Thanksgiving craft using your toddler's tiny handprint. This craft is simple to do, and your toddler can decorate it however they'd like. These handprint crafts make great table decorations for Thanksgiving dinner!

STEPS

1. Trace your child's hand onto a piece of card stock paper with a crayon or marker. On the bottom of the hand, draw a vertical rectangle. Have your child color their traced hand with crayons or markers.

2. The thumb will be the face. Help your child glue a googly eye onto it and draw a smile and gobbler.

3. Cut out the handprint with the vertical rectangle attached.

4. Bend the rectangle part backwards so the handprint can stand up.

CAUTION *Keep your child away from the scissors.*

RUB A LETTER

MESSINESS

2

PREP TIME

5 minutes

ACTIVITY TIME

10 minutes

MATERIALS

Hot glue gun

Card stock paper

Crayons

PREP

Use a hot glue gun to write letters on card stock paper. Create as many alphabet sheets as you'd like.

STEPS

1. Once the glue has dried, place another piece of paper on top of the alphabet sheet.

2. Have your toddler use crayons to scribble all over the paper.

3. Talk about how the letters show up through the scribbles. Discuss the letters' names and sounds.

CAUTION *Keep your child away from the hot glue gun.*

HOMEMADE WATERCOLORS

MESSINESS

2

PREP TIME

1 hour

ACTIVITY TIME

20 minutes

MATERIALS

3 or 4 jars

Water

Markers, old or new

Cornstarch

Paintbrushes

Paper

PREP

Fill each jar with two tablespoons of water. Place a marker, tip down, into each jar. Let them sit for about one hour to release the colors. Then, add 1 teaspoon of cornstarch to each jar and stir.

STEPS

1. Have your toddler dip a paintbrush into the watercolors and paint the paper.

2. Talk about the different colors and how this paint is much lighter than regular paint.

3

EXPLORE

ODDLERS ARE NATURALLY curious. They love
to test out ideas and get into messy situations.
Even if it looks like your toddler is making a
giant mess, keep in mind that they are also learning. For
example, has your toddler ever emptied out an entire
box of tissues? All three of my boys have done that,

simply because they're curious: What happens when you pull out a tissue? The tissues keep coming and it's hard to stop until they're all gone!

The activities in this chapter are hands-on experiences for exploring the world toddlers live in. Many of the activities are related to simple science concepts because science is all about seeking answers to questions. Some of the activities are messy, so I recommend putting on old clothes and doing the messy activities outdoors.

PICTURE SCAVENGER HUNT

MESSINESS

1

PREP TIME

5 minutes

ACTIVITY TIME

30 minutes

MATERIALS

Camera

Printer

Stapler

PREP

Take photos of places around your home or outside that will be recognizable to your toddler. Good examples are a corner of a room, a special tree, or part of a picture hanging on the wall. Print the pictures and staple them together to make a booklet.

STEPS

1. Look at the photos and talk about where your child thinks each picture was taken.

2. Search inside and outside to find the locations.

3. Once they find the spot from the picture, mark an X on the photo.

APPLES TO APPLESAUCE

MESSINESS

3

PREP TIME

5 minutes

ACTIVITY TIME

**20 minutes
(cooking time 6 hours)**

MATERIALS

5 apples

Vegetable peeler

Apple corer

Knife

Cutting board

Slow cooker

Juice from 1 lemon

**1 tablespoon
brown sugar**

**1 teaspoon
vanilla extract**

**½ teaspoon
ground cinnamon**

¼ cup water

STEPS

1. Have your child hold an apple, and talk about what it looks like and how it feels. Then peel it, core it, and cut it into slices. Eat a slice with your toddler and discuss the texture and taste.

2. Talk about how apples can be used to make other food, such as apple pie, apple cider, caramel apples, and applesauce.

3. Show the apple seeds to your toddler. Discuss how seeds grow into plants and trees. Practice counting the seeds.

4. Have your toddler help you with some of the easy steps for making homemade applesauce, such as measuring ingredients, while you peel, core, and cut up the rest of the apples. Have your child help you transfer the apple pieces from the cutting board into the slow cooker. Add the lemon juice, brown sugar, vanilla, cinnamon, and water. Mix it all up and cook on low for 6 hours.

5. When the applesauce is ready, enjoy a bowl of it!

6. Talk about the difference in taste from the plain apple and warm applesauce.

CAUTION *Keep your child away from the vegetable peeler and knife.*

COLORED LEAVES

MESSINESS

1

PREP TIME

None

ACTIVITY TIME

**10 minutes
(2 days of observation)**

MATERIALS

Green leaf

Scissors

Bowl

Water

Red food coloring

Magnifying glass
(optional)

STEPS

1. Have your child pick a green leaf with a stem.

2. Snip off a small piece of the stem and place the leaf in a bowl of water, then add a few drops of red food coloring.

3. Leave the leaf in the water for two days.

4. Observe how the leaf's veins and stem change to the color red.

5. Use a magnifying glass to see it up close.

6. Discuss how this shows how a leaf gets water. The stem and veins are important for carrying water and minerals to the whole leaf to keep it alive.

CAUTION *Keep your child away from the scissors.*

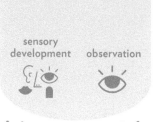
DANCING POPCORN KERNELS

MESSINESS

2

PREP TIME

None

ACTIVITY TIME

15 minutes

MATERIALS

Water

Clear jar

**1 tablespoon
popcorn kernels**

2 tablets Alka-Seltzer

STEPS

1. Have your toddler pour water into the jar until it is three-quarters full.

2. Next, they should add the popcorn kernels. Notice how the kernels sink to the bottom of the jar.

3. Break one Alka-Seltzer tablet into four small pieces. Have your toddler add the four pieces to the jar. At first you won't see much beyond bubbles.

4. Break the second tablet into four small pieces. Add these pieces to the jar. This time, watch how the bubbles make the kernels dance around the jar.

5. The kernels will move around for 10 to 15 minutes. If they slow down and you want to see them move again, simply add another tablet.

FLOATING BALL

MESSINESS

2

PREP TIME

None

ACTIVITY TIME

10 minutes

MATERIALS

Paper cup

Scissors

Bendable straw

Pom-pom

Tape

STEPS

1. Poke a small hole in the bottom of the paper cup with the scissors.

2. Bend the straw and poke the shorter side of the straw into the hole. Tape the straw in place.

3. Place a pom-pom in the cup.

4. Have your toddler blow air into the cup through the straw.

5. Watch how the pom-pom floats up when air is pushed out of the straw.

6. See how long your toddler can keep the ball up before it falls.

CAUTION *Keep your child away from the scissors.*

STICKY NATURE CUFF

MESSINESS

2

PREP TIME

5 minutes

ACTIVITY TIME

20 minutes

MATERIALS

Scissors

Toilet paper roll

Contact paper

Objects from nature

PREP

Cut a toilet paper roll to make it lie open. Cut a piece of contact paper to fit onto the outside of the roll. Place the sticky side out and tape the ends to the cuff.

STEPS

1. Place the cuff on your child's wrist.

2. Go on a walk and collect items from nature.

3. Stick the items onto the cuff.

4. When you get home, observe all the items you collected and talk about what each item feels like, smells like, and looks like.

CAUTION *Keep your child away from the scissors.*

* SKILLS LEARNED *

POM-POM COLOR DROP

MESSINESS
2

PREP TIME
5 minutes

ACTIVITY TIME
20 minutes

MATERIALS
Paper towel rolls

Markers

Masking tape

Small bowls

Colorful pom-poms

Large bowl

PREP

Draw a line of color on the top of a paper towel roll with a marker. Repeat this with a different color on another roll; do this with multiple colors and multiple rolls. Tape the paper towel rolls to the wall using masking tape and place a small bowl underneath each one. Pour colorful pom-poms into a larger bowl.

STEPS

1. Let your child choose a pom-pom from the large bowl and find the paper towel tube that matches the color of the pom-pom.

2. Have your toddler place the pom-pom in the tube and watch it drop through.

3. Continue doing this until all the pom-poms are sorted by color.

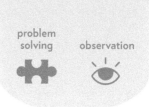
BALANCE THE TOYS

MESSINESS

2

PREP TIME

5 minutes

ACTIVITY TIME

10 minutes

MATERIALS

Hole punch

2 paper cups

Scissors

String

**Plastic hanger
with notches**

Small toys

PREP

Use a hole punch to make a hole on both sides of a paper cup. Cut a piece of string, about 12 inches long. Tie the ends of the string to the holes in the cup. Repeat these steps to make a second cup.

Place the strings on the notches of the hanger, so the cups hang down like buckets. Place the hanger somewhere where it can swing easily and is at the child's height.

STEPS

1. Have your toddler gather small toys from around the house. The toys could be Legos, small figurines, blocks, etc.

2. Ask your child to place the toys in the cups. Notice how one side hangs lower than the other side. Talk about how the lower side weighs more.

3. Continue to fill the cups with different items, and observe how the scale changes.

4. Challenge your toddler to make the cups balance.

CAUTION *Keep your child away from the scissors.*

GARDEN IN A BAG

MESSINESS
2

PREP TIME
None

ACTIVITY TIME
20 minutes, plus 7 days for observation

MATERIALS
Gallon-size plastic zip-top bag

Markers

Paper towels

Water

Flower seeds

Tape

STEPS

1. Have your toddler draw a garden scene onto the plastic bag with the markers. This could consist of grass, flowers, and trees.

2. Wet several paper towels and wring them out so they are damp but not wet.

3. Lay the paper towels flat and put 3 or 4 seeds onto them, making sure they are spaced apart. Fold the paper towels in half.

4. Place the paper towels at the bottom of the bag and seal the bag most of the way, leaving a little bit open on one side.

5. Tape the bag to a window with sunlight.

6. Observe the bag over the next seven days, and watch the seeds sprout. After the seeds have germinated, transfer them to soil.

MY BODY

MESSINESS

3

PREP TIME

None

ACTIVITY TIME

20 minutes

MATERIALS

Roll of paper

Marker

Washable paint

Paintbrush

STEPS

1. Roll the paper onto the floor and have your toddler lie on it.

2. Trace around your toddler's body with the marker.

3. Help your child draw a face on the body and talk about the parts of the face.

4. Talk about how the drawing is the size of your toddler. Use their feet to measure how tall they are. Count the number of steps they take.

5. Have your toddler use paint to color in the body.

6. After it dries, hang up the body painting for all to see.

SHAKE IT UP

MESSINESS

1

PREP TIME

None

ACTIVITY TIME

10 minutes

MATERIALS

Mason jar

Water

Food coloring

Vegetable oil

STEPS

1. Have your toddler help you fill a Mason jar halfway with water and drop in a few drops of food coloring.

2. Help your child pour vegetable oil in the jar until it reaches the top, and then screw on the lid.

3. Let your toddler shake the jar for 5 seconds. Then watch the jar while counting to 20. After about 20 seconds, the two mixtures will settle; the oil will remain on top, while the water stays on the bottom. Talk about how water and oil never mix.

4. Continue to shake the jar and see how the two liquids never mix together.

FIZZY COLOR BURST

MESSINESS

4

PREP TIME

5 minutes

ACTIVITY TIME

20 minutes

MATERIALS

Muffin tin

Food coloring

Baking soda

White vinegar

Bowl

Large tray

**Dropper or
plastic syringe**

PREP

Place a few drops of food coloring in each compartment of the muffin tin. Cover each color up with 1 tablespoon of baking soda. Pour vinegar into a bowl next to the muffin tin. Place everything on top of a large tray.

STEPS

1. Have your toddler fill a dropper or syringe with vinegar.

2. Squeeze the vinegar into each compartment of the muffin tin.

3. Watch as the color is revealed when the two materials react and bubble up.

4. Talk about the names of each color.

BLIZZARD IN A JAR

MESSINESS

2

PREP TIME

None

ACTIVITY TIME

20 minutes

MATERIALS

Clear jar

Baby oil

Small bowl

½ cup very warm water

½ teaspoon white paint

Alka-Seltzer tablets

STEPS

1. Have your toddler carefully fill the jar three-quarters full of baby oil.

2. In a small bowl, mix together the water with the white paint. Pour this mixture into the jar of baby oil.

3. After the white water and oil separate, add a tablet of Alka-Seltzer.

4. Watch as the materials inside the jar react to the Alka-Seltzer. You should see a blizzard. When it dies down, add another tablet.

COFFEE FILTER PARACHUTE

MESSINESS

2

PREP TIME

5 minutes

ACTIVITY TIME

10 minutes

MATERIALS

Scissors

Thin string or floss

Lego figurine or something similar in size

Coffee filter

Tape

PREP

Cut two pieces of string or floss into 12-inch-long pieces. Tie each piece of string onto an arm of the figurine. Make sure the arm lands in the middle of the string. Pull the ends of the strings on each arm toward the coffee filter. Tape each end of the string to the inside of the coffee filter, near the top. Make sure the four string pieces are spaced out evenly so the figurine is level.

STEPS

1. Send your child to a safe high place, such as the top of the stairs. They should hold the coffee filter and then release the parachute.

2. Watch how the parachute slows down the speed of the falling figurine.

3. Try releasing the figurine at different heights to see if the height changes how it falls.

CAUTION *Keep your child away from the scissors.*

DINOSAUR FOSSILS

MESSINESS

3

PREP TIME

None

ACTIVITY TIME

**1 hour 15 minutes,
including cooking time**

MATERIALS

4 cups flour

1 cup salt

Bowl

1½ cups water

Spatula

Cookie sheet

Plastic dinosaur toys

STEPS

1. Preheat the oven to 350°F.

2. Have your toddler help you make the dough. First, pour the flour and the salt together into a bowl.

3. Slowly pour water into the bowl while stirring with the spatula.

4. Grease the cookie sheet, then pour the dough mixture onto it and spread it out.

5. Have your toddler take plastic dinosaurs and stamp them into the dough to make imprints. Remove the dinosaurs.

6. After the dough is covered in prints, place it in the oven at 350°F for 45 minutes.

7. When it's done, let it cool.

8. Observe the different fossil imprints and talk about their differences.

CAUTION *Keep your child away from the oven.*

HOMEMADE RIVER

MESSINESS

3

PREP TIME

5 minutes

ACTIVITY TIME

15 minutes

MATERIALS

Aluminum foil

Dish soap

Garden hose

Toy boats

TIP *If the boat gets stuck, encourage your toddler to problem solve before fixing it yourself.*

PREP

Find a place on a hill or on a sloped driveway to create your aluminum river. Tear off a piece of aluminum foil, about three feet long. Fold the edges of the foil inward to keep the water from spilling out. Use your hand to press down in the middle to eliminate bumps. Squirt a few drops of dish soap on the tin foil. Put the foil river on the hill or driveway and place a hose at the top of the river.

STEPS

1. Have your toddler turn the hose on so water flows down the river.

2. Let your toddler send boats and other toys down the river.

COLOR BOOK FROM NATURE

MESSINESS

1

PREP TIME

5 minutes

ACTIVITY TIME

20 minutes

MATERIALS

Colored construction paper in black, brown, white, red, orange, yellow, green, blue, and purple

Stapler

Tape

PREP

Stack different colors of construction paper together and fold the stack down the middle. Staple the papers along the folded side to create a book.

STEPS

1. Go on a walk with your toddler. When your toddler finds an interesting item from nature, have them tape it to the matching colored paper.

2. After the walk, go over the items found and taped in the color book. Talk about the different colors and names of the items.

CAUTION *Keep your child away from the stapler.*

APPLE VOLCANO

MESSINESS

4

PREP TIME

5 minutes

ACTIVITY TIME

15 minutes

MATERIALS

Apple

Knife

Tray

Baking soda

Food coloring

Vinegar

Dropper or spoon

PREP

Core an apple and scrape away some of the apple flesh inside to make a hole.

STEPS

1. Put the apple on a tray. Have your toddler fill the hole inside the apple with a few scoops of baking soda.

2. Add a few drops of food coloring.

3. Fill a dropper with vinegar and let your toddler slowly add it to the apple.

4. Watch as the reaction causes an eruption, similar to a volcano.

5. Poke holes in the sides of the apple and watch the eruption seep out the top and the sides.

6. Continue to put baking soda and vinegar inside the apple to watch it erupt again.

CAUTION *Keep your child away from the knife.*

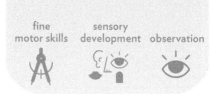

fine
motor skills

sensory
development

observation

• SKILLS LEARNED •

EXPLORING SEEDS

MESSINESS

3

PREP TIME

None

ACTIVITY TIME

20 minutes

MATERIALS

Fruit or vegetables with seeds, like bell peppers, pumpkins, cucumbers, pears, apples, watermelons, and cantaloupes

Knife

Tweezers

Small bowls

Magnifying glass
(optional)

PREP

Cut open the fruit and vegetables with a knife.

STEPS

1. Let your toddler use tweezers or their hands to remove the seeds and place them into bowls.

2. Discuss the different size, texture, and color of the seeds with your toddler.

3. Eat the fruit and vegetables after taking out the seeds.

CAUTION *Keep your child away from the knife.*

ICE BOATS

MESSINESS

2

PREP TIME

1 hour

ACTIVITY TIME

20 minutes

MATERIALS

Ice cube tray

Water

Straws

Scissors

Paper

Hole punch

Markers

**Large container
of water or bathtub
filled with water**

PREP

Fill the ice cube tray with water. Put in the freezer for 30 minutes. Cut straws in half and place them in the center of each half-frozen ice cube. Place the tray back in the freezer until the water is fully frozen.

STEPS

1. Have your toddler make the sails for the boats. Take a small rectangular piece of paper and punch holes on the top and bottom using a hole punch.

2. When you're ready for the activity, take the ice cube tray out of the freezer. Slide the sails through the straws and pop the ice cubes out of the tray.

3. Let your toddler sail the ice boats in a container of water or a bathtub filled with water.

4. Have your toddler touch the ice and talk about how it feels. Observe how the ice melts in the water after floating for a while.

5. Race the ice cube boats in the activity from Homemade River (page 79).

CAUTION *Keep your child away from
the scissors.*

ANIMAL FEET

MESSINESS

4

PREP TIME

None

ACTIVITY TIME

15 minutes

MATERIALS

Tape

Paper

Washable paint

Paper plates

Plastic animals

PREP

Tape pieces of paper to the table. Pour paint onto paper plates.

STEPS

1. Have your toddler dip a plastic animal's feet into the paint and stamp the feet around the paper.

2. Discuss the differences in the footprints.

hand-eye
coordination

fine
motor skills

dexterity

· SKILLS LEARNED ·

SQUIRT THE BALL

MESSINESS

4

PREP TIME

None

ACTIVITY TIME

15 minutes

MATERIALS

Chalk

Small squirt gun or spray bottle

Water

Ping-pong ball

STEPS

1. Have your child draw a box on the ground using chalk.

2. Let your toddler stand a few feet away from the box and squirt water at a ping-pong ball with the squirt gun to propel it forward.

3. Your toddler should use their hand-eye coordination to guide the ping-pong ball into the boxed area with the squirt gun.

FEELINGS GAME

MESSINESS

1

PREP TIME

5 minutes

ACTIVITY TIME

5 minutes

MATERIALS

Paper plate

Marker

Brad, or any a small bendable nail

Paper clip

PREP

Draw a line from top to bottom and side to side on a paper plate using a marker. In the four sections, draw four faces: happy, sad, angry, and surprised. Poke a small hole in the center of the circle. Poke the brad through the middle of the paper clip, then through the hole. Bend the backside of the brad slightly, making sure the paperclip can spin around easily when flicking it.

STEPS

1. Have your toddler spin the paper clip around.

2. Look at the face the spinner landed on and ask your toddler to mimic that emotion on their face.

3. Talk about the name of the emotion and ask your toddler about a time when they felt that way. (For example, I felt sad when I lost my favorite toy.)

4. If you feel that your toddler is advanced enough, try adding to the game: Make eight sections on the paper plate and draw these faces: happy, sad, angry, surprised, worried, silly, tired, and embarrassed. Repeat the steps above.

MAGNETIC SENSORY BOTTLE

MESSINESS

1

PREP TIME

None

ACTIVITY TIME

10 minutes

MATERIALS

Baby oil

Empty clear plastic water bottle

Metal pieces like pipe cleaners, nuts, washers, and paper clips

Glue

Large magnet

STEPS

1. Pour baby oil into the bottle until it is nearly full.

2. Place metal items into the bottle and seal the lid closed with glue.

3. Have your toddler use the large magnet to move the items around the bottle from the outside.

EGG IN A BOTTLE

MESSINESS

1

PREP TIME

None

ACTIVITY TIME

15 minutes

MATERIALS

Hard-boiled egg

4 cups boiling water

Sturdy clear plastic container with a narrow top
(a juice container works well)

STEPS

1. Peel the boiled egg with your toddler.

2. Pour the boiling water into the empty container (away from your toddler).

3. Right away, have your toddler place the peeled boiled egg on the opening of the bottle so no air can escape.

4. Observe how the egg slowly gets sucked into the bottle.

5. After a couple of minutes, you'll see the egg fully get sucked into the bottle. It may make a loud noise!

CAUTION *Keep your child away from the boiling water.*

fine
motor skills

sensory
development

problem
solving

• SKILLS LEARNED •

NEST BUILDING

MESSINESS

4

PREP TIME

None

ACTIVITY TIME

20 minutes

MATERIALS

Play-Doh

**Materials for making
a nest, like twigs,
hay, or grass**

Toy eggs

STEPS

1. Talk about how a bird gathers materials and weaves
   them together to create a nest.

2. Go outside and help your toddler find materials for
   making a nest.

3. Back inside, mold Play-Doh into a shape like a bowl.
   This will be the base of your toddler's nest.

4. Have your toddler poke the materials they found
   into the Play-Doh to create a nest.

5. Place the pretend eggs inside. Pretend to be birds.

EXPANDING BALLOONS

MESSINESS
2

PREP TIME
None

ACTIVITY TIME
10 minutes

MATERIALS
Balloon

Permanent marker

Funnel

½ cup vinegar

Plastic bottle

2 teaspoons baking soda

STEPS

1. Have your toddler draw a face on the deflated balloon using a permanent marker.

2. Let your toddler help you pour the vinegar into a plastic bottle with a funnel.

3. Stretch the mouth of a balloon over the funnel. Drop the baking soda into the funnel to fill the balloon.

4. Stretch the mouth of the balloon over the top of the bottle and let your toddler lift the balloon up.

5. The baking soda will drop into the bottle. When it hits the vinegar, it will cause a reaction that will fill the balloon with air.

6. Show your toddler the face they drew on the balloon as the balloon grows.

STAMPING BUGS

MESSINESS

2

PREP TIME

None

ACTIVITY TIME

15 minutes

MATERIALS

Play-Doh

Plastic bug toys

STEPS

1. Have your toddler roll the Play-Doh into a ball, then press down on the ball to flatten it.

2. Let your toddler stamp a plastic bug toy in the Play-Doh.

3. Pull the bug off and observe the imprint.

4. Do this with several kinds of bugs and observe the differences in the patterns.

DIRT JARS

MESSINESS

1

PREP TIME

None

ACTIVITY TIME

10 minutes

MATERIALS

Dirt

Mason jar with a lid

Water

STEPS

1. Have your toddler collect a handful of dirt from outdoors and place it in a jar.

2. Add water to the jar until it reaches the top. Screw on the lid.

3. Shake the bottle and set it down.

4. Watch how the dirt particles slowly fall to the bottom.

5. Discuss how the dirt is heavier than water, which causes it to sink.

Pumpkin Boats

MESSINESS

3

PREP TIME

5 minutes

ACTIVITY TIME

20 minutes

MATERIALS

Knife

Miniature pumpkins

Spoon

Large container filled with water

Small toys

Pumpkins are everywhere during the fall months. There are so many ways to use pumpkins, but one way for toddlers to enjoy them is by turning them into boats. This is a fun way to explore buoyancy!

PREP

Cut the miniature pumpkins in half. Scoop out the pumpkin guts and seeds with a spoon.

STEPS

1. Have your child place the pumpkin boats into a container with water.

2. Ask your child to add toy people or animals to the boats.

3. See how much the boat can hold before it sinks. Let your toddler fill the boat with different items: acorns, rocks, pom-poms, or water.

TIP *Try playing with pumpkin boats in the bathtub!*

CAUTION *Keep your child away from the knife.*

fine
motor skills

oral motor
development

dexterity

• SKILLS LEARNED •

PUMP IT UP

MESSINESS

2

PREP TIME

5 minutes

ACTIVITY TIME

20 minutes

MATERIALS

Masking tape

Large pom-pom

Empty water sprayer

Straw

PREP

Make a long track on the floor with masking tape.

STEPS

1. Have your child place a pom-pom in front of the sprayer and use the air from the sprayer to move the pom-pom down the track.

2. Get your toddler to try using a straw to propel the pom-pom forward with air.

3. Talk about which tool moved the pom-pom down the track more easily.

MAKE A SPLASH

MESSINESS

4

PREP TIME

5 minutes

ACTIVITY TIME

15 minutes

MATERIALS

Large container

Water

Small items like feathers, rocks, acorns, leaves, and small toys.

Towel

Chair or stool

PREP

Fill a container with water. Set the items on a towel. Place a chair or stool next to the container.

STEPS

1. Help your toddler gather small items with a little weight from around the house or outside.

2. Before your toddler drops each item in the water, ask them to guess if it will make a splash.

3. Have your toddler drop each item into the water and observe if it made no splash, a little splash, or a big splash.

4. If your toddler is stable on a chair, have them stand on a chair or stool, hold their hand, and have them drop items into the water. Ask if this height changed the amount of splashing.

SALT WATER EXPERIMENT

MESSINESS
1

PREP TIME
None

ACTIVITY TIME
15 minutes

MATERIALS
4 glasses

Water

4 raw eggs

Salt

Spoon

STEPS

1. Fill the glasses with water.

2. Have your toddler gently place one egg in the first glass of water. Observe what happens.

3. Pour 1 tablespoon of salt into the second glass of water and stir. Place an egg in the glass.

4. Pour ¼ cup salt into the third cup of water and stir. Place an egg inside it.

5. Pour ½ cup salt into the fourth cup of water and stir. Place an egg inside it.

6. Observe what happens with the different cups of water. Talk about how salt makes the egg float.

MOVING WATER

MESSINESS

3

PREP TIME

None

ACTIVITY TIME

20 minutes

MATERIALS

2 bowls

Water

Small cups

Large plastic tub

Tools to gather water, like basters, droppers, sponges, spoons, and plastic syringes

STEPS

1. Place a bowl of water, an empty bowl, and small cups in a large plastic tub.

2. Invite your toddler to use the tools to transfer the water from one bowl to another.

3. Encourage your toddler to try all the tools and observe how they carry the water differently.

fizzy stars

MESSINESS

3

PREP TIME

1 hour, including freezer time

ACTIVITY TIME

20 minutes

MATERIALS

1 cup water

½ cup baking soda

Bowl

Food coloring

Star-shaped ice cube tray

Plate

Vinegar

Dropper

Celebrate the 4th of July with this fizzy ice stars activity. Just like fireworks, this activity is sure to excite your toddler. In a few simple steps, your child will get to observe the bubbly and fizzing ice stars.

PREP

Mix the water with the baking soda in a bowl. Add a few drops of food coloring and stir. (To make red, white, and blue colors, separate the baking soda and water mixture into three bowls before adding food coloring.) Next, pour the mixture into the ice cube tray. (You may have to scoop in the baking soda, since it tends to sit at the bottom of the mixture.) Put it in the freezer until the mixture is frozen.

STEPS

1. Pop the stars out of the ice cube tray and place them on the plate.

2. Fill a dropper with vinegar.

3. Have your toddler squeeze the vinegar onto the stars and watch them fizz.

4. Listen to the fizzy sound they make.

MAGNET HANDS

MESSINESS

2

PREP TIME

5 minutes

ACTIVITY TIME

15 minutes

MATERIALS

Hot glue gun

Small magnets

Mitten

Bin

Rice or dry beans

Metal items like alphabet magnets, washers, paper clips, and cut-up pipe cleaners

PREP

Use a hot glue gun to attach small magnets to a mitten.

STEPS

1. Fill a bin with rice or dry beans and add the magnetic items.

2. Place the mitten on your toddler's hand.

3. Have your toddler move their hand around in the bin and then pull it up.

4. Observe which items stuck to the magnets. If your child pulls up an alphabet letter, talk about the letter name.

CAUTION *Keep your child away from the hot glue gun and be sure that your child does not put any item in their mouth.*

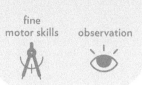
TOWERS AND SHADOWS

MESSINESS

2

PREP TIME

None

ACTIVITY TIME

2 hours and 10 minutes

MATERIALS

Craft paper

Plastic or wood blocks

Markers

STEPS

1. Place a large piece of craft paper on the ground outside.

2. Have your toddler build a structure using blocks.

3. Draw the shadow of the structure on the piece of paper using a marker. Have your toddler help with this as much as possible.

4. Wait one hour and look at how the shadow changed. Draw the outline using a different colored marker.

5. Wait another hour and draw the outline again.

6. Observe how the sun moves during the day and changes where the shadows are.

TOSS THE BALLOON

MESSINESS

2

PREP TIME

10 minutes

ACTIVITY TIME

20 minutes

MATERIALS

Funnel

Balloons

Flour

Dry beans

Rice

Water beads

Sand

Play-Doh

PREP

Use a funnel to add different materials to as many balloons as you would like. Make sure to leave one empty. Blow them all up and tie them shut.

STEPS

1. Have your toddler take a balloon and toss it into the air.

2. Ask your child to toss all the balloons and talk about the differences in how they feel.

3. Play a tossing game. Take one balloon and stand with feet together and facing each other. Toss the balloon.

4. Take one step back and toss the balloon again.

5. Keep going until you can't catch the balloon anymore.

6. Repeat this game with the different weighted balloons.

4

PRETEND

PRETEND PLAY IS a healthy part of a child's social, emotional, and cognitive development. When I think of toddlers, one of the first things that comes to mind is their love for pretend play. They love to play make-believe with dolls and stuffed animals, dress up in costumes, and have races with their toy vehicles.

During pretend play, toddlers are learning what people are like, how people think, and what people do. This helps children understand themselves and the world they live in. A study done by Dr. Alison Gopnik found that pretend play leads to better social adjustment in school and social competence in life. Parents who expose children to flash cards are doing less to help their children academically than parents who expose their children to pretend play, read to them, and talk with them.

The activities in this chapter are designed to encourage dramatic play. Some activities involve creating props for imaginary play, which takes time to prepare but allows for more time for free play. The other activities invite children to a specific pretend play activity. Toddlers love it when you are playful and silly with them, so make sure to play alongside them.

GLACIER ANIMALS

MESSINESS

2

PREP TIME

**1 hour, including
freezer time**

ACTIVITY TIME

20 minutes

MATERIALS

Small containers

Water

Sink filled with water

**Small plastic glacier
animals like penguins,
polar bears, and seals**

Small plastic fish

PREP

Fill small containers with water. Place them in the
freezer. When you are ready for the activity, take them
out and allow a few minutes for them to thaw. Pop
the ice out of the containers. Fill a plugged-up sink
with water. Place the ice blocks in the sink and add the
plastic animals. Put small fish in the water for the glacier
animals to hunt and gather.

STEPS

1. Let your toddler play with the animals and pretend
   they live on the glacier.

2. Have the animals swim, play with other animals, and
   hunt for fish.

   TIP *You can also use pieces of Styrofoam
   to mimic the glaciers.*

HUNGRY FISH

MESSINESS

2

PREP TIME

5 minutes

ACTIVITY TIME

15 minutes

MATERIALS

Tennis ball
(low compression)

Knife

Hot glue gun

2 pom-poms

2 googly eyes

PREP

Cut a line on the ball using a knife to make the mouth of a fish. Hot-glue the pom-poms above the mouth. Glue googly eyes on top of the pom-poms.

STEPS

1. Show your toddler how to squeeze the sides of the ball to open the mouth.

2. Have your child feed pom-poms to the fish until it is full.

3. Squeeze the sides of the ball to open the mouth and dump out the pom-poms.

4. Pretend that the fish is hungry and wants to eat the pom-poms until its mouth is full.

CAUTION *Keep your child away from the hot glue gun and knife.*

STORY ROCKS

MESSINESS

1

PREP TIME

1 hour, including
drying time

ACTIVITY TIME

15 minutes

MATERIALS

10 to 20 smooth rocks

White spray paint

Permanent markers

Basket

PREP

Gather the rocks. Spray-paint the top of the rocks white. Once the rocks have dried, draw designs such as the sun, moon, people, flowers, animals, trees, and rivers on the rocks with markers. Place them in a basket.

STEPS

1. Have your toddler choose a rock from the basket. Start a story based on the rock that your toddler picked.

2. Choose another rock and add another part to the story.

3. Take turns choosing a rock and adding parts to the story.

CAUTION *Keep your child away from the spray paint.*

TIP *To save time, just add stickers to the rocks.*

BUNNY FINGER PUPPET

MESSINESS

2

PREP TIME

5 minutes

ACTIVITY TIME

15 minutes

MATERIALS

White card stock paper

Scissors

Large round hole punch
(optional)

1 white pipe cleaner

Glue

2 googly eyes

Pink and black crayons

1 white pom-pom

PREP

Cut a small oval from the card stock paper. Make two round holes near the bottom of the oval for your child's fingers. You can do this with scissors or a large round hole punch. Bend a white pipe cleaner to look like bunny ears. Glue the ears to the top backside of the bunny. Glue on the googly eyes. Draw a nose with the pink crayon and a mouth with the black crayon. Glue the white pom-pom to the side to look like a bunny's tail.

STEPS

1. Place your toddler's pointer and middle fingers in the round holes.

2. Show your child how to make the bunny hop around using their arm.

3. Create two bunnies and pretend to be bunny friends hopping around the garden.

CAUTION *Keep your child away from the scissors.*

BABY BED

MESSINESS

2

PREP TIME

5 minutes

ACTIVITY TIME

20 minutes

MATERIALS

Glue

Cotton balls

Scissors

Fabric

Shoe box

Stickers

Crayons

Baby doll

PREP

Glue a handful of cotton balls together to make a pillow. Cut a piece of fabric to create a blanket. Place both inside the shoe box.

STEPS

1. Have your toddler decorate the outside of the box with stickers or crayons.

2. Let your toddler place the baby doll in the box and tuck the doll into bed.

CAUTION *Keep your child away from the scissors.*

CARDBOARD COMPUTER

MESSINESS

1

PREP TIME

15 minutes

ACTIVITY TIME

15 minutes

MATERIALS

24" x 12" piece of cardboard

Glue

White paper

Black marker

PREP

Bend the cardboard in half so the top part becomes the monitor and the bottom becomes the keyboard, similar to a laptop. Glue a white piece of paper to the top piece to make the monitor. Outline it in black marker. Glue a white piece of paper to the bottom section for the keyboard. Draw the keyboard using a marker.

Optional: You can use letter stickers for the keyboard buttons. You can also print a picture from a website and glue that onto the monitor.

STEPS

1. Have your toddler pretend to type on the computer.

2. Ask your toddler to find a letter or number on the keyboard to practice recognition.

FAIRY WINGS

MESSINESS

3

PREP TIME

5 minutes

ACTIVITY TIME

20 minutes

MATERIALS

Marker

Large foam sheet

Scissors

Clear contact paper

Sequins

Glitter

Hole punch

Yarn or string

PREP

Draw an outline of fairy wings onto the foam sheet. Make a 1-inch border. Cut out the wings so it just leaves the border. Place the border of the wings onto a large piece of clear contact paper.

STEPS

1. Have your toddler sprinkle sequins and glitter onto the contact paper within the border you created.

2. Place another piece of contact paper on top to seal everything in.

3. Cut around it, making sure to leave a small border of contact paper so it will stay sealed.

4. In the center of the wings, make a hole in the top and bottom with a hole punch.

5. Cut two long pieces of string and thread one piece of string through the top hole, leaving enough length for your child to put their arms through it, and then tie it to the bottom hole. Repeat this step so you have two straps.

6. Place the wings on your toddler and let them fly around like a fairy!

CAUTION *Keep your child away from the scissors.*

SUPER HERO CUFFS

MESSINESS

1

PREP TIME

None

ACTIVITY TIME

10 minutes

MATERIALS

Scissors

Toilet paper rolls

**Markers, crayons,
and stickers**

STEPS

1. Cut each toilet paper roll lengthwise to make it lie open.

2. Have your toddler decorate the outside of the toilet paper rolls with markers, crayons, and stickers to make them look like super hero cuffs.

3. Slip the rolls onto your toddler's wrists and have them pretend to be a super hero.

CAUTION *Keep your child away from the scissors.*

FLOWER GARDEN

MESSINESS

5

PREP TIME

5 minutes

ACTIVITY TIME

20 minutes

MATERIALS

Soil

Plastic bin

Artificial flowers

Rocks

Seeds

Small shovels

Flower pots

PREP

Pour the soil into the bin.

STEPS

1. Encourage your child to use their hands to feel the soil. If they are sensitive to getting their hands dirty, give them gloves.

2. Let your toddler create a flower garden inside the bin with the artificial flowers, rocks, seeds, and shovels, or have them scoop up the dirt into a pot, and "plant" the artificial flowers.

CROWN

MESSINESS

3

PREP TIME

None

ACTIVITY TIME

**30 minutes,
including drying time**

MATERIALS

**Paint
Paintbrushes
Paper plate
Scissors
Stickers**

STEPS

1. Have your toddler paint a paper plate. Allow time to dry.

2. Place the plate facedown and poke a hole in the middle of it using scissors.

3. From the hole in the middle of the plate, cut a straight line toward the rim, stopping about 1 inch from the edge.

4. From the point in the middle, angle the scissors slightly to the right and cut toward the rim, again stopping about 1 inch from the edge. This will make a triangle shape.

5. Help your toddler bend the triangle so it stands up.

6. Continue cutting out triangles around the plate until you have eight.

7. Have your toddler add stickers or other decorations to the crown, and help them put it on their head. Then, let them pretend to be a king, queen, prince, princess, or any sort of pretend royalty they choose! You can even make a second crown for yourself so you can be part of their royal court!

CAUTION *Keep your child away from the scissors.*

HOMEMADE DRUM

MESSINESS

2

PREP TIME

5 minutes

ACTIVITY TIME

15 minutes

MATERIALS

Paper

Hot glue gun

Large empty canister with a lid
(hot chocolate containers work well)

Bells

Crayons

Markers

Stickers

Drumsticks
(optional)

PREP

Glue paper to the sides of the canister. Glue bells to the drum to make a jingle sound when your toddler hits it.

STEPS

1. Have your toddler draw on the drum with crayons or markers or decorate it with stickers.

2. Invite them to bang the drum using their hands or drumsticks.

3. Talk about the sounds they hear. Encourage your toddler to make a variety of sounds with the drum.

4. Tap a rhythm on the drum and have your toddler repeat the rhythm.

5. Turn on music and encourage your toddler to drum to the music.

CAUTION *Keep your child away from the hot glue gun.*

PIG SNOUTS

MESSINESS

2

PREP TIME

10 minutes

ACTIVITY TIME

10 minutes

MATERIALS

Scissors

Styrofoam cup

Pink sock

Markers

Elastic string

Stapler

PREP

Cut a large hole in the bottom of a Styrofoam cup. Make sure the hole is big because you want good airflow for this mask. Wrap the pink sock around the cup and draw two holes for the pig nostrils. Take the sock off and cut out the holes. Place the sock back on the cup. Measure your child's head with a piece of elastic string. Staple that elastic string to the inside of the cup.

STEPS

1. Place the pig snout on your toddler.

2. Show your child how to act and sound like a pig.

CAUTION *Keep your child away from the scissors and stapler.*

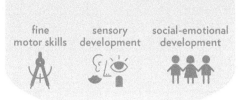

fine
motor skills

sensory
development

social-emotional
development

• SKILLS LEARNED •

DOLL WASHING STATION

MESSINESS

4

PREP TIME

5 minutes

ACTIVITY TIME

30 minutes

MATERIALS

Water

2 plastic bins

Bubble bath soap

Baby doll

Old toothbrush

Washcloth

Squirt bottle

Small towel

PREP

Pour water into both plastic bins. Add bubble bath soap to the second bin.

STEPS

1. Help your toddler undress the baby doll and set the clothes aside.

2. Rinse the baby in the water bin.

3. Place the baby in the bubble bath bin.

4. Let your toddler use an old toothbrush and washcloth to scrub the baby clean.

5. Rinse the baby with clean water using a squirt bottle.

6. Dry off the baby with a towel.

7. Let your child repeat the activity with multiple baby dolls.

PILLOWCASE COSTUME

MESSINESS

1

PREP TIME

5 minutes

ACTIVITY TIME

15 minutes

MATERIALS

Scissors

Old pillowcase

Markers

Sequins

Pom-poms

Glue

PREP

Cut a hole at the top of the pillowcase large enough to fit around your toddler's head. Measure where their arms will go and cut out holes.

STEPS

1. Have your toddler color the pillowcase with markers or decorate it with sequins and pom-poms. They can also make it look like their favorite animal.

2. Cut strips at the bottom of the pillowcase to make a fringe hem.

3. Have your toddler wear the pillowcase as a costume and act out their character.

CAUTION *Keep your child away from the scissors.*

fine
motor skills

social-emotional
development

communication

• SKILLS LEARNED •

DOG AND CAT MASK

MESSINESS

2

PREP TIME

5 minutes

ACTIVITY TIME

20 minutes

MATERIALS

Scissors

2 paper plates

Glue

1 wide craft stick

Colored paper

Strips of gray yarn

Strips of brown yarn

PREP

Cut out the center of both paper plates, leaving just the rim. Throw away the centers. Glue a wide craft stick to the bottom of one paper plate for your toddler to hold. Glue the backsides of the paper plates together. Cut out pointy cat ears from paper. Glue them to one side of the paper plate. Cut round dog ears from the paper. Glue them to the opposite side of the paper.

STEPS

1. Have your toddler make glue dots around the cat side of the paper plate and lay gray yarn onto the glue for cat hair. It doesn't need to be in any certain order.

2. Flip the plate over. Have your toddler make glue dots around the dog side of the paper plate and lay brown yarn on the glue.

3. Once the mask is dry, let your toddler pretend to be a cat or dog with the mask.

CAUTION *Keep your child away from the scissors.*

ELEPHANT FEET

MESSINESS

3

PREP TIME

None

ACTIVITY TIME

**1 hour, including
drying time**

MATERIALS

Glue

2 empty tissue boxes

**Gray tissue paper
squares or gray paper**

Scissors

**White paper or
foam sheet**

STEPS

1. Spread glue around the outside of the tissue boxes.

2. Stick gray tissue paper squares to the glue. Involve your toddler as much as you can to help them work on fine motor skills.

3. Cut three circles from the white paper or foam sheets. Cut the three circles in half to create six elephant toes.

4. Glue three toes to the front of each box.

5. Wait for the boxes to dry.

6. Place your toddler's feet into the boxes.

7. Watch your toddler walk and stomp around like an elephant!

CAUTION *Keep your child away from the scissors.*

fine
motor skills

numbers

oral motor
development

123

* SKILLS LEARNED *

BIRTHDAY DOUGH

MESSINESS

4

PREP TIME

None

ACTIVITY TIME

20 minutes

MATERIALS

Roller
Play-Doh
Plastic knife
Birthday candles

STEPS

1. Have your toddler roll Play-Doh and mold it to look like a birthday cake.

2. Place unlit candles into the Play-Doh. Ask your toddler to count the candles and then pretend to blow them out.

3. Help your toddler make different kinds of Play-Doh cakes with different numbers of candles to work on counting.

FEED THE ALLIGATOR

MESSINESS

2

PREP TIME

5 minutes

ACTIVITY TIME

20 minutes

MATERIALS

Glue

2 pom-poms

Plastic container with a flap lid
(such as a dishwashing detergent pellet box)

2 googly eyes

Ping pong balls

Basket

Large tongs

PREP

Glue two pom-poms onto the top flap of the container to create alligator eyes. Glue one googly eye onto each pom-pom. Place the ping-pong balls into a basket.

STEPS

1. Have your toddler feed the alligator by using the tongs to pick up the ping-pong balls, lift the lid, and drop the balls into the container.

2. See if your toddler can feed the alligator without dropping any of the ping-pong balls.

apple picking

MESSINESS

2

PREP TIME

5 minutes

ACTIVITY TIME

15 minutes

MATERIALS

Scissors

Clear contact paper

Tape

Permanent marker

Paper apples of assorted colors

Fall is the perfect time to go apple picking. And apple picking helps your toddler work on counting, sorting, and colors!

PREP

Cut out a large piece of contact paper. Tape it to a wall or window so the sticky side is facing out. Draw a tree outline on the sticky part. Place paper apple cutouts near the tree.

STEPS

1. Have your toddler place the paper apples on the tree.

2. Ask your toddler to count how many apples can fit on the tree.

3. To work on listening skills and recognizing colors, ask your toddler to follow your directions. For example, tell them to place three yellow apples on the tree and two red apples on the ground.

CAUTION *Keep your child away from the scissors.*

FIRE RESCUE

MESSINESS

5

PREP TIME

None

ACTIVITY TIME

20 minutes

MATERIALS

Lego Duplo blocks
(or something similar)

Plastic bin

Shaving cream

**Red and yellow
food coloring**

Squeeze bottle

Warm water

STEPS

1. Build a house with Lego Duplo blocks.

2. Set the house in a plastic bin.

3. Squirt shaving cream around the house.

4. Squeeze a few drops of red and yellow food coloring onto the shaving cream to make it look like a fire.

5. Ask your toddler to pretend to be a firefighter and put out the fire using the squeeze bottles full of warm water.

6. Have them squeeze the bottle of water onto the toy and continue squirting until all the shaving cream has been washed away.

RAINBOW FISH

MESSINESS

2

PREP TIME

None

ACTIVITY TIME

15 minutes

MATERIALS

Large sock

Dry beans

2 googly eyes

Glue

Markers

STEPS

1. Have your toddler fill a sock with dry beans. Tie it with a knot. Glue the googly eyes on the opposite end.

2. Ask your toddler to draw a face and rainbow-colored gills onto the stuffed sock.

3. Let your toddler play with their rainbow fish toy.

4. For gross motor skills, practice tossing the fish back and forth with your child or have your child throw it into a basket.

BUG HUNT

MESSINESS

1

PREP TIME

5 minutes

ACTIVITY TIME

15 minutes

MATERIALS

Plastic toy bugs
Magnifying glass

PREP

Hide plastic bugs around your home.

STEPS

1. Pretend to be on a bug hunt with your toddler. Look around your home for the plastic bugs.

2. Use a magnifying glass to find the bugs or to look closer at the bugs.

TIP *Sing this chant while you hunt:*

We're going on a bug hunt! (repeat)
We don't know what we'll find. (repeat)
Let's look and find the next one,
We'll hunt until we're done!

RIBBON TWIRLERS

MESSINESS

1

PREP TIME

5 minutes

ACTIVITY TIME

10 minutes

MATERIALS

Scissors

Ribbon

Hot glue gun

Wooden dowel rod

PREP

Cut a piece of ribbon three feet long. Glue it to the end of a wooden dowel rod.

STEPS

1. Have your toddler hold the wooden dowel rod and move the ribbon in the air.

2. Ask your child to twirl around, shake the dowel rod, and make a figure eight motion in the air.

3. Turn on music to dance with your toddler as they twirl the ribbon.

CAUTION *Keep your child away from the scissors and hot glue gun.*

JET PACKS

MESSINESS

2

PREP TIME

5 minutes

ACTIVITY TIME

20 minutes

MATERIALS

Empty clear large plastic juice bottle

Scissors

Colored tissue paper

Hot glue gun

Elastic string

PREP

Remove the label from the juice bottle. Cut tissue paper to look like flames and glue them to the bottom of the bottle. Cut two pieces of elastic string about 1 foot long each, and glue the ends of them to the bottle using a hot glue gun to create straps.

STEPS

1. Have your toddler stuff tissue paper into the container to fill it and make it look colorful.

2. Place the jet pack on your toddler's back and encourage them to pretend they are flying around.

CAUTION *Keep your child away from the scissors and hot glue gun.*

PET GROOMING SALON

MESSINESS

3

PREP TIME

None

ACTIVITY TIME

20 minutes

MATERIALS

Stuffed animals

Plastic bins

Empty shampoo bottles

Towel

Brushes

Pipe cleaners

STEPS

1. Have your toddler give the stuffed animals in their pet salon a pretend (dry) bath in one of the bins with the empty bottle of shampoo.

2. Let your child groom the animals by drying them off with a towel and brushing their fur.

3. Add a collar to the pets by twisting a pipe cleaner around their neck.

HISSING SNAKES

MESSINESS

2

PREP TIME

5 minutes

ACTIVITY TIME

15 minutes

MATERIALS

White socks

Scissors

Red pipe cleaners

Googly eyes

Glue

Markers

PREP

Poke a small hole at the bottom of a sock. Cut a red pipe cleaner about 2 inches long for the tongue. Place a small part of it inside the hole and bend it so it stays in place and won't poke your child's hand. (Tape it if it won't stay on its own.) Glue on 2 googly eyes.

STEPS

1. Have your toddler decorate the snake puppet using markers.

2. Place the snake on your child's hand and arm.

3. Let your toddler hiss and pretend to slither around like a snake.

4. Help your child make more snakes to play with each other.

CAUTION *Keep your child away from the scissors.*

LION MASK

MESSINESS

3

PREP TIME

5 minutes

ACTIVITY TIME

20 minutes

MATERIALS

Scissors

Paper plate

Yellow yarn

Yellow paper

Glue

Yellow washable paint

Paintbrush

Elastic string

Stapler

PREP

Make holes in the plate for the eyes. Cut yellow yarn into 2-inch pieces. Make two ears using yellow paper and glue them to the plate.

STEPS

1. Paint the paper plate yellow.

2. After the paint dries, glue the yellow yarn to the rim of the paper plate to look like a lion's mane.

3. Measure your child's head and cut a piece of elastic string to that size. Staple it to the plate.

4. Have your child try on the lion mask and pretend to roar and move like a lion!

CAUTION *Keep your child away from the scissors and stapler.*

YOGA ANIMAL POSES

MESSINESS

1

PREP TIME

None

ACTIVITY TIME

15 minutes

MATERIALS

Mat
(optional)

STEPS

1. Put a mat on the ground if using one. Have your child use their body to create yoga poses that look like animals. Start by having them place both hands on the ground while raising their bottom into the air, like the downward dog pose.

2. Next, they should come down to a plank on their hands and toes like an alligator.

3. Ask them to get down on all fours, tuck their chin into their chest, and round their back. Encourage them to roar like a tiger.

4. Have your child sit on their heels and bring their forehead down to the floor. They should rest their arms alongside their body to look like a turtle.

5. Next, they should lie on their stomach and place their palms flat next to their shoulders. Have them press into their hands to lift their shoulders and head off the ground, then hiss and pretend to be a snake.

6. Finally, have them squat with their knees apart and their arms between their knees, then press their hands together and croak like a frog.

HOMEMADE TRUMPET

MESSINESS

1

PREP TIME

5 minutes

ACTIVITY TIME

10 minutes

MATERIALS

Pencil

Paper towel tube

Paper bowl

Scissors

PREP

Trace the end of a paper towel tube onto the bottom of the paper bowl. Cut around the circle in the bowl to create a hole. Place the paper towel tube into the hole with the bowl facing out. This helps amplify the sound.

STEPS

1. Place the trumpet up to your toddler's mouth and have them make noises.

2. Listen to the sounds the trumpet makes.

3. Have your toddler try a whispered sound and then a loud sound. Talk about the differences.

CAUTION *Keep your child away from the scissors.*

POST OFFICE MAILBOX

MESSINESS

2

PREP TIME

10 minutes

ACTIVITY TIME

30 minutes

MATERIALS

Tape

Medium cardboard box

Utility knife

Marker

Pipe cleaner

Paper

Writing utensils

PREP

Tape the box closed so there are no open sides. Use a utility knife to cut a 5-inch-long mailbox slot near the top of the box. Toward the bottom of the box, use the utility knife to make a circle shape, leaving a quarter of the cardboard intact as a hinge, to create a door to collect the mail. Make two small holes toward the top of the door. Poke a pipe cleaner through one side and out the other side to make a handle. Tape the ends inside the lid so the pipe cleaner stays in place.

STEPS

1. Have your toddler pretend to write letters to friends and family. Scribbling is encouraged at this age!

2. Stick the letters in the mailbox.

3. When your child is done mailing letters, they can gather the letters from the door of the mailbox.

CAUTION *Keep your child away from the utility knife.*

HARVEST SENSORY BIN

MESSINESS

4

PREP TIME

5 minutes

ACTIVITY TIME

20 minutes

MATERIALS

**2 to 3 cups
popcorn kernels**

Plastic bin

Small play pumpkins

**Toy tractors
with trailers**

**Child-safe garden
equipment, such as
plastic shovels,
rakes, etc.**

PREP

Pour the popcorn kernels into a plastic bin.
Add pumpkins, tractors, and shovels.

STEPS

1. Invite your toddler to play with the harvest bin.

2. Encourage your child to scoop up the kernels
   and pumpkins and place them in the trailers.

3. Ask your toddler to try scooping the kernels
   with their hands, or use a small rake to comb
   through them.

CAUTION *Don't do this activity with
children who like putting objects in
their mouths.*

ICE CREAM SHOP SENSORY BIN

MESSINESS

3

PREP TIME

None

ACTIVITY TIME

20 minutes

MATERIALS

**Pom-poms or
cotton balls**

Plastic bin

Scooper

Spoons

Play ice cream cones

Bowls

Sequins

STEPS

1. Have your toddler place pom-poms into a bin. Add a scooper, spoons, play ice cream cones, and bowls.

2. Have your toddler scoop the pom-poms and place them on the cones or in bowls.

3. Suggest that your child sprinkle sequins on top of the pom-poms for the topping.

4. Pretend to eat the ice cream with your toddler.

CAUTION *Don't do this activity with children who like putting objects in their mouths.*

ZOO ANIMAL CAGES

MESSINESS

2

PREP TIME

10 minutes

ACTIVITY TIME

20 minutes

MATERIALS

Small cardboard boxes

Scissors

Elastic string

Stapler

Colored paper
(optional)

Glue
(optional)

Stuffed animals

Bowls

PREP

Remove the cardboard box tops. Cut four or five pieces of elastic string and staple them onto each box to make them look like cages. Have your toddler glue colored paper to the sides if they want to add color.

STEPS

1. Have your toddler place stuffed animals in the cages.

2. Encourage your child to pretend to be a zoo keeper. Let them give the animals bowls of pretend food and water, pretend to bathe them, and put them to sleep in their cages.

CAUTION *Keep your child away from the scissors.*

CLEANING TEETH

MESSINESS

2

PREP TIME

None

ACTIVITY TIME

15 minutes

MATERIALS

Play-Doh

Empty egg carton

String or floss

Toothbrush

STEPS

1. Have your toddler roll 10 small pieces of Play-Doh into 10 small snakes.

2. Turn the egg carton upside down. Help your child place the Play-Doh pieces in between each compartment.

3. Pretend that the egg carton compartments are teeth and the Play-Doh pieces are food. Help your toddler use a piece of string or floss to remove the Play-Doh. You may have to help your toddler move the string around to be able to do this.

4. If the floss is too challenging, try using a toothbrush.

5. Talk about the importance of brushing and flossing teeth.

SHOWER CURTAIN HULA SKIRT

MESSINESS

1

PREP TIME

10 minutes

ACTIVITY TIME

20 minutes

MATERIALS

Scissors

Plastic shower curtain

Velcro fasteners with sticky backs

Jewels
(optional)

Glue
(optional)

PREP

Cut the shower curtain to the width of your toddler's waist. Also cut the curtain to the length that you want. Then cut 2-inch-wide strips into the shower curtain, stopping about 4 inches from the top. Attach the Velcro fasteners to each side. Glue jewels to the top of the skirt to decorate it.

STEPS

1. Wrap the hula skirt around your toddler and let them pretend to be a hula dancer.

2. Have your toddler twirl around and watch the edges of the skirt float up.

CAUTION *Keep your child away from the scissors.*

mummy stuffed Animals

MESSINESS

4

PREP TIME

None

ACTIVITY TIME

10 minutes

MATERIALS

Toilet paper
Stuffed animals

Your toddler can turn their stuffed animals into spooky creatures during the Halloween season. This simple play and pretend activity is fun for kids and reinforces hand-eye coordination and hand strength.

STEPS

1. Have your toddler wrap toilet paper around their stuffed animals, leaving the eyes exposed to make them look like mummies.

2. After wrapping the stuffed animals up into mummies and playing with them, get your toddler to rip off the toilet paper layers from the dolls to work on hand strength.

3. Help your child gather the toilet paper pieces, press them together to make balls, and throw them into the trash.

BABY CARRIER

MESSINESS

1

PREP TIME

15 minutes

ACTIVITY TIME

15 minutes

MATERIALS

**Child-size
long-sleeved shirt**

Ruler

Scissors

Baby doll

PREP

1. Lay the shirt flat on the ground. Measure 2 inches in from the left side of the shirt. Cut up the shirt, about 5 inches high. Repeat for the right side.

2. Tie the right-side sleeve to the cut you made on the right side. Tie the left sleeve to the left piece you cut.

3. Cut the remaining middle part of the shirt into four equal vertical flaps, with the cuts being about 5 inches high.

4. Tie the left two pieces together and the right two pieces together. This will be the spot where the doll's legs go.

continued

BABY CARRIER *continued*

STEPS

1. Place the doll inside the carrier, putting its legs through the slots.
2. Slide the carrier onto your toddler's arms so the baby rests on their chest.
3. Encourage your toddler to pretend to be the baby's parent.

CAUTION *Keep your child away from the scissors.*

FROG HOPPING

MESSINESS

2

PREP TIME

5 minutes

ACTIVITY TIME

15 minutes

MATERIALS

Scissors

Green foam sheets

Marker

PREP

Cut green foam sheets to look like lily pads. Write numbers on them. Place them around the room.

STEPS

1. Have your child pretend to be a frog and jump onto the lily pads without stepping in the water (the floor).

2. Say a number and have your toddler find the number and hop to that lily pad.

3. If your toddler doesn't know the number, show them the number to help them learn it.

CAUTION *Keep your child away from the scissors.*

MUDDY VEHICLES

MESSINESS

5

PREP TIME

5 minutes

ACTIVITY TIME

15 minutes

MATERIALS

Shaving cream

Tray

Brown food coloring

Container

Water

Toy trucks and cars

PREP

Spray shaving cream onto a tray. Mix in brown food coloring (or mix several colors of food coloring to make brown). Fill a container with water and set it next to the tray.

STEPS

1. Have your child play with toy trucks and cars in the shaving cream tray. Pretend that the vehicles are getting muddy.

2. Let your child wash off the vehicles in the container of water.

fine
motor skills

sensory
development

social-emotional
development

• SKILLS LEARNED •

DOLL CASTS

MESSINESS

4

PREP TIME

None

ACTIVITY TIME

**20 minutes and
overnight for drying**

MATERIALS

Newspaper

Gauze

½ cup flour

½ cup warm water

Bowl

Whisk

Plastic baby dolls

PREP

Cover the table you are working on with newspaper.
Tear gauze into small strips.

STEPS

1. Have your child help you mix the flour with the warm
   water in a bowl. Use the whisk to remove lumps.

2. Show your toddler how to dip the gauze into the
   mixture to coat it well. Use your fingers to remove
   excess liquid (since this will be too difficult for
   a toddler).

3. Help your child wrap the strips around the doll's
   arms, legs, or head to create a bandage.

4. Keep adding the damp gauze until the doll's pretend
   wound is covered well.

5. Let the bandages dry overnight.

6. When your toddler wants to remove the cast, they
   can simply pull the gauze off with their fingers.

LIGHT SWORD

MESSINESS

1

PREP TIME

10 minutes

ACTIVITY TIME

10 minutes

MATERIALS

Pool noodle

Serrated knife

Silver duct tape

Black permanent marker

Small flashlight

PREP

Cut a pool noodle in half with the serrated knife. Tape duct tape around the bottom of the noodle to create a handle. Use a marker to draw on/off buttons onto the duct tape. Turn on a flashlight and poke it into the open end of the noodle. If it does not seem secure, use more tape so it does not fly out during play.

STEPS

1. Have your child pretend to have a duel with their light sword.

2. Take your toddler into a dark room and let them move the light sword. Watch how the light moves around the wall.

CAUTION *Keep your child away from the knife and make sure the flashlight is wedged tight inside the pool noodle so it doesn't slip out.*

OUTDOOR CAR WASH

MESSINESS
5

PREP TIME
10 minutes

ACTIVITY TIME
30 minutes

MATERIALS
Scissors

Shower curtain

Wooden dowel rod

2 chairs

2 buckets

Water

Dish soap

Toy vehicles

Sponge

Towel

PREP

Cut a shower curtain in half so it is shorter than usual. Then, cut 3-inch-wide strips in the shower curtain from the bottom up to 5 inches away from the top. Poke a wooden dowel rod through the holes at the top of the shower curtain. Rest the ends of the rod on two chairs. Fill one bucket with water and the other bucket with soapy water.

STEPS

1. Have your toddler listen to and follow these car wash steps: Rinse the car in the bucket of water. Use a sponge to scrub the car with soapy water. Roll the car through the shower curtain. Rinse it again with water. Dry it with a towel.

2. Repeat to wash more cars.

CAUTION *Keep your child away from the scissors.*

5

SENSE

FROM BIRTH, CHILDREN learn about their world using their five senses: seeing, smelling, hearing, touching, and tasting. As they grow, their senses are their most familiar and basic way to explore and process new information. Sensory play enhances learning through hands-on activities that stimulate your child's senses. This is a great way for children to explore the world they live in!

Sensory play supports language development, cognitive growth, fine and gross motor skills, problem solving, and social interaction. It even helps build their vocabulary. For example, when a child uses Play-Doh, they learn that it feels "squishy" and "soft." In addition, sensory play activities can help calm a child who may be anxious or frustrated. Children enjoy these types of activities because they can be creative while engaging their senses.

SQUISHY BAGS

MESSINESS

1

PREP TIME

5 minutes

ACTIVITY TIME

15 minutes

MATERIALS

10 gallon-size plastic zip-top bags

Water

Gel

Soap

Shaving cream

Coconut oil

PREP

Pour water into the first bag, and seal it. Place it into another bag to make sure the contents don't spill out. Then seal the outer bag. Repeat this with the gel, soap, shaving cream, and coconut oil.

STEPS

1. Give your toddler the squishy bags. Allow time for them to explore how each bag feels.

2. Set the bags on the table and let your toddler use their finger to draw pictures or make letters on the bags.

3. Talk about the senses your toddler is experiencing. Be sure to mention scent, touch, and sound.

BATH BOMBS

MESSINESS

2

PREP TIME

None

ACTIVITY TIME

2 hours 30 minutes, including drying time

MATERIALS

1 cup baking soda

½ cup citric acid

½ cup Epsom salts

Large bowl

Small bowl

2 teaspoons olive oil

1 teaspoon water

Whisk

Food coloring

Essential oils
(optional)

Muffin tin

Bathtub

PREP

Mix the baking soda, citric acid, and Epsom salts in a large bowl. In a small bowl, mix together the olive oil, water, and food coloring. If you want scented bath bombs, add a couple drops of essential oils, such as lavender or sweet orange, to the liquid bowl.

Pour in 1 teaspoon of the liquid material to the dry mixture and mix with a whisk. Continue adding in liquid until it is all mixed in.

Pack the mixture down tightly in the muffin tin molds. Allow the mixture to sit for 1 hour. Use a table knife to lift the bath bombs out of the muffin tin. Flip them over and wait another hour for the other side to dry.

STEPS

1. Remove the bath bombs from the molds and place them in the bathtub with your toddler.

2. Watch and listen as the bath bombs fizz and make a hissing sound.

3. Have your toddler hold the bath bomb in their hands while it is fizzing. Talk about how it feels, smells, and sounds.

fine
motor skills

sensory
development

gross
motor skills

• SKILLS LEARNED •

MILK CONTAINER SHAKER

MESSINESS

1

PREP TIME

None

ACTIVITY TIME

10 minutes

MATERIALS

Pom-poms

Empty plastic milk jug

STEPS

1. With your toddler, place pom-poms into the milk jug.

2. Place the lid onto the jug and then ask your toddler to shake the jug up and down. Listen to the sound it makes as your toddler shakes it.

3. Have your child shake it slowly and quietly and then shake it fast to make it louder.

4. Let your toddler toss the jug in the air and then try to catch it, or gently pass the jug to each other.

MUDDY FARM ANIMALS

MESSINESS

5

PREP TIME

5 minutes

ACTIVITY TIME

20 minutes

MATERIALS

Towel

Plastic bin

Chocolate pudding

Shredded wheat cereal

Plastic farm animals

Container of water

PREP

Lay a towel down and set a plastic bin onto it. Pour the chocolate pudding into one side of the bin to create a mud pile. On the other side, place shredded wheat cereal to represent hay. Place the animals in the bin. Fill a container with water and set it next to the bin.

STEPS

1. Have your child play with the farm animals, rolling them around in the chocolate pudding to get them muddy and rinsing them clean in the water.

2. Let your child use the cereal as hay to feed the animals or for the animals to climb on.

GEL BAG

MESSINESS

1

PREP TIME

5 minutes

ACTIVITY TIME

10 minutes

MATERIALS

Hair gel

Gallon-size plastic zip-top bag

Photograph that you don't mind getting dirty

Tape

PREP

Pour hair gel into a bag until the bag is about halfway full and seal it tightly. Tape a picture on the table. Place the bag on top of the picture and tape the bag to the table.

STEPS

1. Have your toddler use their fingers to move the hair gel around.

2. Tell your child to move the hair gel around until they can figure out what the picture is underneath.

3. Keep playing with the bag by creating pictures, writing numbers or letters, or drawing shapes on the gel bag.

SHAKER TEST

MESSINESS

2

PREP TIME

5 minutes

ACTIVITY TIME

10 minutes

MATERIALS

4 to 6 paper plates

Items to be used as fillers for the shakers: dry beans, rice, noodles, pom-poms, bolts and washers, yarn pieces, pipe cleaner pieces, Q-tips, etc.

Stapler

PREP

Fill one paper plate with a filler. Place an upside-down paper plate on top and staple the plates together, leaving no space for the filler to fall out and creating a pocket for the filler to move around in. Repeat to create more shakers.

STEPS

1. Invite your toddler to hold the shaker and move it around to create sound.

2. Let your child try all the shakers and talk about the different sounds each one makes.

3. Ask your toddler to sort the shakers by quiet sounds and loud sounds.

4. Show your child how to make a rhythmic pattern such as loud, soft, loud, soft.

GUESSING GAME

MESSINESS

1

PREP TIME

5 minutes

ACTIVITY TIME

10 minutes

MATERIALS

5 tissue boxes
Small ball
Piece of fabric
Rock
Pinecone
Feather

PREP

Place one item from the Materials list in each tissue box.

STEPS

1. Have your toddler place one hand into a tissue box. Ask them to feel around and guess what the item is without looking at it.

2. Encourage them to describe how it feels to them.

3. Once they make a guess, lift the item out of the box and see if they are right.

4. Repeat this with all boxes.

SCENT JARS

MESSINESS

1

PREP TIME

5 minutes

ACTIVITY TIME

10 minutes

MATERIALS

Small jars with lids, like salt and pepper shakers or small Mason jars

Scented liquids, such as coffee, vanilla extract, peppermint extract, orange juice, dish soap, or hot chocolate

PREP

Put a little of each scented liquid into each jar. Place the lids on the jars.

STEPS

1. Give your toddler a jar. Take off the lid and have them smell what's inside.

2. Ask your toddler to guess what the smell is and encourage them to use descriptive words.

3. After they guess, tell them what it is.

4. Let your toddler smell all the jars and choose their favorite scent.

OCEAN SENSORY TRAY

MESSINESS

3

PREP TIME

30 minutes plus overnight in the refrigerator

ACTIVITY TIME

20 minutes

MATERIALS

3-ounce box of blue Jell-O

Aluminum baking sheet

Brown sugar

Whipped cream

Octopus candy

Red fish candy

Goldfish crackers

Container of water

Towel

PREP

Prepare the Jell-O according to the package directions. Pour it into the aluminum baking sheet and let it set overnight in the refrigerator. The next day, take the Jell-O out of the refrigerator and start to assemble all the ingredients on top of it. Spread brown sugar on one side of the baking sheet for the sand. Squeeze some whipped cream in rows to make the white-capped waves. Then sprinkle the candies and goldfish crackers around in the Jell-O ocean.

STEPS

1. Invite your toddler to play with the ocean sensory tray.

2. Encourage them to use their hands to play in the ocean; have water and a towel nearby to clean their hands.

3. Let your child squish the Jell-O in their hands and talk how about how it feels cold, slimy, and smooth. Have them smell it and even taste the contents on the tray!

FRUITY SCENTED DOUGH

MESSINESS

2

PREP TIME

15 minutes

ACTIVITY TIME

15 minutes

MATERIALS

1 cup flour + extra for kneading

1 cup water

¼ cup salt

2 teaspoons vegetable oil

1 tablespoon cream of tartar

3-ounce box of fruit-flavored Jell-O

Pot

Spatula

Silicone baking mat

Rolling pin

Cookie cutters

PREP

In a medium pot, mix the flour, water, salt, vegetable oil, cream of tartar, and Jell-O together. Cook over medium-low heat for a few minutes, stirring constantly with a spatula. Once the dough gathers in the center of the pot, remove it from the heat and set it on a mat. Let it cool for a minute, then knead it with some flour. Repeat these steps with different flavors of Jell-O to make multiple scents and colors.

STEPS

1. With your toddler, squish the Play-Doh and talk about how it feels and smells.

2. Roll it, mold it, cut it into shapes with cookie cutters, and shape it into balls or snakes.

3. When your toddler is done playing, store it in an airtight container for up to four weeks.

STARRY NIGHT

MESSINESS

2

PREP TIME

10 minutes

ACTIVITY TIME

15 minutes

MATERIALS

Large cardboard box
(at least 20″ x 20″ x 15″)

Scissors

**Multicolored
Christmas lights**

PREP

Poke holes in the top of a cardboard box using scissors. Stick the lights into the holes (facing into the box) and turn the lights on.

STEPS

1. Invite your toddler into the starry box and have them look at the color lights.

2. Talk about the colors of the lights.

3. Turn off the room lights and watch how the Christmas lights get brighter.

CAUTION *Keep your child away from the scissors.*

SWAMPLAND

MESSINESS

5

PREP TIME

25 minutes

ACTIVITY TIME

20 minutes

MATERIALS

½ cup chia seeds

Large bowl

4 cups water

Green food coloring

Spoon

Plastic bin

Plastic swamp animals, e.g., frogs, alligators, fish, snakes, insects, etc.

Rocks and sticks

PREP

Pour the chia seeds into a large bowl. Add in 2 cups of the water and 10 drops of food coloring. Stir the mixture with a spoon. Let it sit for 20 minutes. Next, pour the green chia seeds into a plastic bin. Add 2 cups of water to the mixture and stir. Set plastic swamp animals around the bin.

STEPS

1. Invite your toddler to feel the chia mixture. Talk about the texture and appearance.

2. Play with the bin and pretend it is a swamp habitat for the animals.

3. Give your toddler rocks and sticks and ask them to create homes in the swamp for the different animals.

4. Have the animals swim, lay on the rocks, and play in their homes.

NOTE *If played with right away, the food coloring does not tend to stain; however, the longer it sits, the more likely it is to stain hands.*

CAUTION *Dispose of the chia seed mixture in the garbage, since chia seeds can expand and clog a drain.*

NATURE SOUP

MESSINESS

3

PREP TIME

None

ACTIVITY TIME

20 minutes

MATERIALS

Items from nature, such as flower petals, pinecones, grass, or leaves

Water

Large bowl

Spoon

STEPS

1. Go on a nature walk and collect items for the soup with your toddler.

2. Pour water into a large bowl. Empty the contents from the nature walk into the bowl.

3. Look at the nature soup and invite your child to smell it. (Petals should give the nature soup a good smell.)

4. Talk about how the soup smells and looks.

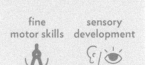
SCENTED FINGER PAINTS

MESSINESS

5

PREP TIME

10 minutes

ACTIVITY TIME

20 minutes

MATERIALS

1 cup flour

2 cups water

Pot

Whisk

Spatula

3 bowls

1 teaspoon vanilla

1 teaspoon cinnamon

1½ teaspoons nutmeg

Paper

Paintbrush
(optional)

PREP

Pour the flour and the water into a pot. Cook over medium heat while stirring with a whisk to eliminate lumps. After about 5 minutes, the mixture will look like a thick paste and clump together. Remove the pot from the stove. Divide the mixture into three bowls using a spatula. Mix the vanilla into one bowl, the cinnamon into the second bowl, and the nutmeg into the third bowl. Wait until the paints have cooled down.

STEPS

1. Show the paints to your toddler and smell them. Talk about the scents and ask which scents they like.

2. Have your toddler dip their finger into the paint and spread it across the paper.

3. Let your toddler create abstract art with the finger paint. If they are reluctant to use their fingers, they can try painting with a paintbrush.

fine
motor skills

sensory
development

counting

• SKILLS LEARNED •

MUDDY INSECTS

MESSINESS

5

PREP TIME

5 minutes

ACTIVITY TIME

20 minutes

MATERIALS

**Brown or gray
food coloring**

Bowl

2 cups baking soda

⅔ cup water

Spatula

Plastic toy insects

Container of water

Tray

Kid tweezers

PREP

Place a few drops of brown food coloring in the bottom of the empty bowl. If you don't have brown food coloring, use 2 drops each of red, green, and blue food coloring to create a gray-brown color. Pour the baking soda and water into the container and mix with the spatula. The consistency should be like mud. Add plastic insects. Set the bowl and the container of water on a tray.

STEPS

1. Show your toddler how to play with the insects in the mud.

2. Have them pick the insects up with tweezers and clean them off in the container of water.

3. After your toddler gets all the insects out of the mud, help them count how many they have.

LOUD VS. QUIET

MESSINESS

2

PREP TIME

10 minutes

ACTIVITY TIME

10 minutes

MATERIALS

Small Mason jars

Items to fill the jars, like Q-tips, pom-poms, kernels, sand, rocks, and nails

PREP

Place each item in a separate jar and screw the lid on.

STEPS

1. Show your toddler how to shake the jars. Talk about the sounds they hear.

2. Have your child sort the jars by loud sounds and quiet sounds.

3. Talk about which sounds your toddler enjoys and which ones they dislike.

fine
motor skills

sensory
development

counting

• SKILLS LEARNED •

SAND SLIME

MESSINESS

3

PREP TIME

5 minutes

ACTIVITY TIME

20 minutes

MATERIALS

Large bowl

Spatula

4 ounces clear glue

¼ teaspoon baking soda

¼ cup fine sand

2 tablespoons saline solution

Shells

PREP

In a large bowl, use the spatula to mix the glue with the baking soda. Stir in the sand. Slowly pour in the saline solution. Keep mixing until the slime has formed.

STEPS

1. Place saline solution on your hands, and on your toddler's hands, and knead the slime until it is a smooth consistency. If it's too sticky, add more saline solution.

2. Have your toddler play with the slime. Talk about how the slime feels on their hands.

3. Help your toddler pull the slime outward to see how far it can stretch.

4. Place shells in the slime and have your child practice counting them.

MUSICAL GLASSES

MESSINESS

2

PREP TIME

5 minutes

ACTIVITY TIME

15 minutes

MATERIALS

8 or more glasses

Water

Food coloring
(optional)

Spoon

PREP

Fill the glasses with different amounts of water, roughly "tuning" them to a major scale (do-re-mi-fa-so-la-ti-do). Place the glasses in order from least to most water, like a xylophone. Add food coloring to the water if you wish.

STEPS

1. Ask your toddler to predict what will happen when they tap the glasses with a spoon.

2. Show your toddler how to tap the glass gently.

3. Allow time for your toddler to explore the different sounds made from the glasses.

4. Play a simple song with the sounds, such as "Hot Cross Buns."

PAINTING SLIPPERY NOODLES

MESSINESS
5

PREP TIME
30 minutes

ACTIVITY TIME
20 minutes

MATERIALS
Spaghetti noodles

Plastic bin

1 teaspoon olive oil

2 cups water

1 cup flour

Pot

Whisk

Bowls

Food coloring

Paintbrushes

PREP

Cook spaghetti noodles according to the package directions. After you drain the noodles, rinse them with cold water. Transfer the noodles into a plastic bin and stir in the olive oil to keep the noodles from sticking to each other.

To make the paint, pour the water and flour into a pot. Mix well with a whisk. Cook on medium heat for a few minutes, until the mixture thickens like paste. Remove from the heat and divide into several bowls. Stir in the food coloring. Allow time to cool before using the paint.

STEPS

1. Place your toddler's hands in the noodles. Talk about how they feel: squishy, soft, warm, or cold. Give your toddler a noodle to eat and talk about how it tastes.

2. Let your toddler use the paint to color the noodles, spreading it with a paintbrush or their fingers.

MOVING CHOCOLATE

MESSINESS

4

PREP TIME

None

ACTIVITY TIME

15 minutes

MATERIALS

½ cup cocoa powder

1½ cups cornstarch

Spoon

Mixing bowl

**1 cup +
1 tablespoon water**

Bowl of warm water

STEPS

1. Have your toddler pour the cocoa powder and cornstarch into the bowl and mix it together with the spoon.

2. Slowly pour in the water while your toddler continues mixing. The mixture will turn into a state between a liquid and a solid.

3. Set it on a table and watch it slowly move. Let your toddler pick it up and notice how it feels like a solid but runs through their fingers.

4. If your toddler's hands get too messy, dip them into the bowl of warm water.

* SKILLS LEARNED *

TRICK YOUR TONGUE

MESSINESS

1

PREP TIME

None

ACTIVITY TIME

10 minutes

MATERIALS

Knife

Apple

Vanilla extract

Cotton balls

Mint leaves

PREP

Cut an apple into slices. Pour a few drops of vanilla extract onto a cotton ball.

STEPS

1. Give your toddler an apple slice to eat. Talk about what it tastes like.

2. Have them smell the vanilla-scented cotton ball. Hold the cotton ball next to their nose while they eat another bite of an apple. Ask your toddler what they taste. (The bite should taste like vanilla.)

3. Now try the same thing with mint leaves. (The apple should taste minty.)

CAUTION *Keep your child away from the knife.*

SENSORY WALK

MESSINESS

5

PREP TIME

5 minutes

ACTIVITY TIME

15 minutes

MATERIALS

5 or more plastic bins

Items to put in the plastic bins, like shaving cream, water beads, sand, water, cornmeal, dry beans, and feathers

Towels

PREP

Fill the plastic bins with items to help your toddler explore the sense of touch. Set the bins in a line outside. If your child needs to clean their feet before stepping into another bin (after stepping in shaving cream, for example), you may want to set out a bin of water and a towel.

STEPS

1. Invite your toddler to step in the bins and feel the different materials with their feet. Hold your toddler's hand in case the material is slippery.

2. After going through the line, go back to the beginning and try it again.

3. Ask your toddler what material was their favorite and least favorite to feel.

fine
motor skills

sensory
development

sorting

* SKILLS LEARNED *

TEXTURE BALLOON

MESSINESS

2

PREP TIME

5 minutes

ACTIVITY TIME

10 minutes

MATERIALS

Funnel

6 balloons

Items to fill the balloon with such as oatmeal, dry beans, rice, flour, honey, water, salt, and soap

2 large buckets

PREP

Use a funnel to fill the balloons. Pour in the filler and then tie the balloon shut. Repeat with other fillers to make 6 or more balloons.

STEPS

1. Have your toddler feel and squeeze all the balloons. Talk about how the balloons feel.

2. Set two buckets a couple of feet away from your toddler.

3. Tell them one bucket is for the soft balloons and the other is for the hard ones.

4. Ask them to feel each balloon, decide if they feel soft or hard, and then toss them into the buckets.

⋅ SKILLS LEARNED ⋅

COCONUT SLIME

MESSINESS

3

PREP TIME

10 minutes

ACTIVITY TIME

15 minutes

MATERIALS

4 ounces clear glue

Bowl

¼ teaspoon baking soda

¼ cup shredded coconut

1 tablespoon saline solution

PREP

Pour the glue in a bowl and mix in the baking soda.

STEPS

1. Let your toddler smell the coconut and help you stir it into the bowl.

2. Slowly pour in the saline solution. Keep mixing until the slime has formed.

3. Pour saline solution on your hands and your toddler's hands and knead the slime until it is a smooth consistency. If it's too sticky, add more saline solution.

4. Have your toddler play with the coconut slime by stretching it, rolling it around, and watching how it moves when they hold it.

5. Talk about how the slime feels on your toddler's hands.

6. Ask your toddler to smell the slime and ask if they like the coconut smell. Discuss the coconut flakes, and how they change the texture of the slime.

HOMEMADE SNOW

MESSINESS

4

PREP TIME

5 minutes

ACTIVITY TIME

15 minutes

MATERIALS

3 cups shaving cream

1½ cups baking soda

Plastic bin

Spoon

**Plastic arctic
toy animals**
(optional)

PREP

Pour the shaving cream and the baking soda into the bin and mix it with the spoon. The homemade snow should be slightly crumbly, but you should be able to mold it into a ball. Place the plastic arctic animals in the snow.

STEPS

1. Invite your toddler to touch the snow. Talk about how it feels.

2. Show them how to gather snow and press it together to create a ball.

3. Encourage pretend play with the arctic animals.

HOT AND COLD JARS

MESSINESS

1

PREP TIME

5 minutes

ACTIVITY TIME

5 minutes

MATERIALS

2 Mason jars
Cold water
Glitter
Hot water

PREP

Fill one Mason jar with cold water, sprinkle in some glitter, and put the lid on. Fill the second Mason jar with hot water, sprinkle in some glitter, and put the lid on.

STEPS

1. Show your toddler the two jars. Have them touch the jars. Discuss how they feel different from each other.

2. Shake the jars and watch the glitter swirl around. Observe the differences between the two jars.

CALMING WATER BIN

MESSINESS

4

PREP TIME

None

ACTIVITY TIME

20 minutes

MATERIALS

Large plastic bin

Water

Purple food coloring
(optional)

**Lavender essential
oil or lavender
bubble bath**

**Bath toys and/or
foam shapes**

Strainer

STEPS

1. Fill a plastic bin with water and add purple food coloring if you wish.

2. Have your toddler drop in lavender essential oil or bubble bath and mix it in with their hands.

3. Have your toddler add the bath toys and shapes, and use the strainer to scoop them up.

LISTENING SCAVENGER HUNT

MESSINESS
1

PREP TIME
5 minutes

ACTIVITY TIME
15 minutes

MATERIALS
Paper
Clipboard
Markers

PREP

Think about the sounds you can hear in your neighborhood. Place a piece of paper in the clipboard, and draw pictures of things you routinely hear, like birds, leaves, water, insects, trains, lawn mowers, kids playing, cars rumbling, airplanes, dogs, and cats.

STEPS

1. Take your toddler outside with your clipboard and listening scavenger hunt paper.

2. Ask your toddler to listen for sounds and mark the ones your toddler hears.

PETAL BATH

MESSINESS
2

PREP TIME
None

ACTIVITY TIME
20 minutes

MATERIALS
Bathtub

**Rose or other
flower petals**

Spoons

Cups

STEPS

1. Help your toddler fill the bath with water and sprinkle in the petals.

2. Tell your child to smell the flowery scents while taking a bath.

3. Suggest that your toddler use spoons to scoop up the petals and place them into cups.

° SKILLS LEARNED °

BUBBLE WRAP ROAD

MESSINESS

3

PREP TIME

5 minutes

ACTIVITY TIME

15 minutes

MATERIALS

Roll of bubble wrap

Masking tape

**Medium or large
toy vehicles**

PREP

Create a road using bubble wrap. Tape the sides to the floor to keep the road in place.

STEPS

1. Help your child roll a vehicle on the bubble wrap road.

2. Listen for the bubble wrap popping and making sounds.

3. Let your toddler crawl on the bubble wrap as they push the vehicle and observe how the bubble wrap pops under their knees.

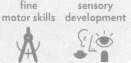
valentine's Day squish Dough

MESSINESS

3

PREP TIME

15 minutes

ACTIVITY TIME

20 minutes

MATERIALS

2 cups water

**2 cups flour + extra
flour for kneading**

½ cup cocoa powder

½ cup salt

**1 tablespoon
cream of tartar**

**2 tablespoons
vegetable oil**

Pot

Whisk

Spoon

Cutting board

Empty chocolate box

It's always fun to receive chocolates on Valentine's Day. Create a pretend chocolate box with this scented chocolate squish dough. Although this activity smells delicious, make sure your toddler doesn't sneak any into their mouth!

PREP

Stir the water, flour, cocoa powder, salt, cream of tartar, and vegetable oil in the pot and cook over medium heat. Stir with the whisk to get clumps out and then switch to stirring with the spoon. Continually stir the mixture for about 10 minutes. Once the dough starts to form a ball and stops sticking to the sides of the pot, you can transfer it to a cutting board sprinkled with flour. Let it cool for a minute, then sprinkle flour on top and knead until the dough is no longer sticky.

STEPS

1. Let your toddler play with the chocolate squish dough. Talk about the scent and how it feels.

2. Help your toddler make pretend chocolates with the squish dough and add them to the chocolate box.

RAIN STICK SENSORY BOTTLE

MESSINESS
2

PREP TIME
None

ACTIVITY TIME
20 minutes

MATERIALS
Small sticks
Plastic water bottle
½ cup uncooked rice
Super Glue

STEPS

1. Go on a nature walk with your toddler and help them find small sticks.

2. Have your toddler place as many sticks as possible inside the bottle.

3. When you return home, pour the rice into the bottle and glue the lid on.

4. Have your toddler tip the bottle upside down and watch how the rice falls. They should move the bottle back and forth and listen to the sound it creates.

CAUTION *Keep your child away from the Super Glue.*

SANDPAPER PICTURES

MESSINESS

2

PREP TIME

None

ACTIVITY TIME

10 minutes

MATERIALS

Tape

Piece of sandpaper

Crayons

STEPS

1. Tape a piece of sandpaper to a table.

2. Let your toddler use the crayons to draw on the sandpaper.

3. Talk with them about how coloring feels different on sandpaper.

JINGLE FEET

MESSINESS

2

PREP TIME

None

ACTIVITY TIME

10 minutes

MATERIALS

10 large craft bells

2 pipe cleaners

PREP

Slide five bells onto a pipe cleaner. Wrap the pipe cleaner around your toddler's ankle and twist the ends together. Repeat to make another one for the opposite ankle.

STEPS

1. Have your toddler move around to explore the sounds of the bells.

2. Ask them to jump, crawl, turn around, shake their feet, and run to hear the sounds they make.

CITRUS PAINT

MESSINESS

3

PREP TIME

10 minutes

ACTIVITY TIME

10 minutes

MATERIALS

1 tablespoon water

Glass bowl

2 tablespoons lemon Jell-O

Spoon

2 teaspoons lemon juice

4 teaspoons flour

Paintbrush

White paper
(card stock works best)

PREP

Pour the water into the bowl. Heat in a microwave for 20 seconds. Add the lemon Jell-O and stir well. Mix in the lemon juice and stir. Add the flour, 1 teaspoon at a time, while stirring thoroughly. Repeat this recipe with lime- or orange-flavored Jell-O to make lime or orange paint, if you wish.

STEPS

1. Have your toddler smell the mixture and talk about the scent.

2. Let your child use the paint to create abstract art.

New Year's Eve Noisemaker

MESSINESS

2

PREP TIME

5 minutes

ACTIVITY TIME

20 minutes

MATERIALS

Aluminum foil

Paper towel tube

Tape

Items to fill the noisemaker: small bells, rice, beans, etc.

Markers

Toddlers love to make noise, so make New Year's Eve a blast with this noisemaker. They can shake it to make a joyous sound to ring in the New Year!

PREP

Tear off a small piece of aluminum foil. Wrap it around one end of the paper towel tube. Add tape around it to keep it in place.

STEPS

1. Have your toddler fill the tube with small items that will make noise. Fill it until the tube is about a third full.

2. Wrap another small piece of aluminum foil over the other end and tape it down.

3. Cover the rest of the tube in aluminum foil and tape it in place. Then write the year on it using marker.

4. Have your toddler shake it and move it back and forth to hear the fun sounds it creates.

GOOGLY EYE BAGS

MESSINESS

1

PREP TIME

5 minutes

ACTIVITY TIME

10 minutes

MATERIALS

**4 gallon-size
plastic zip-top bags**

2 cups water

**1 packet of
googly eyes,
divided in half**

**1 cup clear
liquid soap**

PREP

Fill a bag with 1 cup of the water. Sprinkle in half of the googly eyes and seal the bag. Fill another bag with clear liquid soap, add the googly eyes, and seal. Put another bag around each and seal.

STEPS

1. Have your toddler use their hands to move the googly eyes around in each bag.

2. Observe and talk about the differences between the water and soap bags. Ask your toddler which bag was easier to move the eyes around.

3. Lift the bags and show your child how the googly eyes sink right to the bottom in the water bag but move slowly downward in the soap bag.

FLUFFY SLIME

MESSINESS
4

PREP TIME
10 minutes

ACTIVITY TIME
15 minutes

MATERIALS
3 cups shaving cream

Bowl

½ cup glue

½ teaspoon baking soda

Food coloring

1 tablespoon saline solution

PREP

Pour the shaving cream into the bowl. Mix in the glue and the baking soda. Add a few drops of food coloring and mix well. Slowly pour in the saline solution while stirring.

STEPS

1. Squirt some saline solution on your hands, and on your toddler's hands, and knead the slime until it's no longer sticky.

2. Invite your toddler to play with the slime. Talk about how it feels.

3. Have your toddler try some of these ways to play with the slime: Hide a small toy inside and try to dig it out; place a straw inside the slime and blow air into it to make bubbles; flatten the slime and create prints with cookie cutters.

4. After playing, store the slime in an airtight container for up to one week.

SHIVERY PAINT

MESSINESS

3

PREP TIME

35 minutes, including freezer time

ACTIVITY TIME

15 minutes

MATERIALS

Shaving cream

Ice cube tray

Food coloring

Paintbrush

Paper

PREP

Spray shaving cream into each compartment of an ice cube tray. Add one drop of food coloring to each section and stir. Place the tray in the freezer for 30 minutes.

STEPS

1. Let your toddler dip a paintbrush into the cold shaving cream paint and transfer some paint to a piece of paper.

2. Your toddler should feel how cold the paint is and then use their fingers to paint the paper.

3. Identify the colors on the paper.

SURPRISE ICE EGGS

MESSINESS

3

PREP TIME

**3 hours, including
freezer time**

ACTIVITY TIME

15 minutes

MATERIALS

Water balloons

**Tiny plastic toys like
small balls and
plastic toy animals**

Water

Food coloring
(optional)

Plastic bin

**Squeeze bottles filled
with warm water**

PREP

Stretch the top of one of the balloons with your fingers and place a small toy inside. Repeat for as many balloons as you would like. Fill the balloons with water and a few drops of food coloring, if you wish. Tie the balloons off and place in the freezer. After the balloons are frozen, take them out of the freezer and peel the balloons off the ice inside. Place the ice into a plastic bin. Fill the squeeze bottles with warm water.

STEPS

1. Have your toddler touch the ice eggs and describe how they feel. Ask your toddler what they think is inside of the eggs.

2. Let your toddler use the squeeze bottles to squirt the eggs with warm water and watch how the ice melts away.

3. Once the toy is visible, show your toddler how to use their fingers to pull it out or keep squirting water to release it.

LEMON CLOUD DOUGH

MESSINESS
5

PREP TIME
5 minutes

ACTIVITY TIME
20 minutes

MATERIALS
8 cups flour
Plastic bin
1 lemon
(for juice and zest)
Whisk
1 cup vegetable oil
Spoon
Pie pans
Cups
Bowls

PREP

Pour the flour into a bin. Add the juice of one lemon and mix with a whisk. Pour in the vegetable oil and mix with either a spoon or your hands. Zest the lemon and sprinkle the pieces into the cloud dough.

STEPS

1. Have your toddler smell the lemon cloud dough and feel it with their hands. Talk about the scent and texture of the dough.

2. Have them use their hands to mold and play with the dough. They can pretend to make a lemon pie by pressing the dough into a pie pan.

3. Encourage your toddler to press the dough into the cups and bowls, using them as molds. Discuss how the dough takes on the shape of the mold.

4. After playing, store the dough in an airtight container for up to two weeks.

CALM DOWN SENSORY BOTTLE

MESSINESS

1

PREP TIME

5 minutes

ACTIVITY TIME

10 minutes

MATERIALS

1½ cups water

Microwave-safe measuring cup

6 ounces corn syrup

Whisk

Fine glitter

Empty clear 20-ounce water bottle

Hot glue gun

PREP

Pour the water into a microwave-safe measuring cup. Heat in the microwave for 2 minutes. Quickly add the corn syrup to the water and whisk together. Pour in a handful of fine glitter and mix. Pour the mixture into the water bottle. Place hot glue around the rim of the bottle and screw the lid on. Give the bottle a few shakes and then let it sit for a few minutes to cool down.

STEPS

1. Show your toddler how to shake the bottle so that the glitter floats.

2. Have your child try rolling the bottle or shaking it fast and slow. Talk about your observations.

CAUTION *Keep your child away from the hot glue gun.*

6

PLAY

PLAY IS VERY important for a toddler's brain development. Activities that emphasize play are vital for your toddler's physical, cognitive, social, and emotional development. Children are naturally drawn to play activities because they are fun! As I've shown through the activities in this book, playing is also a wonderful time for learning and a special time to bond with your child.

Some of the activities in this chapter are invitations to play, which means you prepare the activity and invite your child to play without any specific instructions. The others are games, which have directions and work on skills like colors, letters, and shapes. A few of the activities ask you to use masking tape on the floor. Before doing this step, test a small area of your floor with the tape to make sure the tape won't ruin it. You may substitute painter's tape or drafting tape, which both are designed to protect surfaces, but note they are not as strong as masking tape and may loosen during play.

COLOR THE SIDEWALK

MESSINESS

5

PREP TIME

5 minutes

ACTIVITY TIME

20 minutes

]MATERIALS

¼ cup flour

Bowl

**5 tablespoons
warm water**

Whisk

Food coloring

Spoon

Paintbrush

PREP

To make the sidewalk paint, pour the flour into a bowl. Slowly add the warm water while stirring with a whisk.

STEPS

1. Help your toddler add 1 or 2 drops of food coloring and stir with a spoon. Repeat the recipe to create more colors.

2. Invite your toddler to paint designs onto the sidewalk with a paintbrush.

3. After they are finished decorating the sidewalk, be sure to wash away the paint with water right away so the sidewalk isn't temporarily stained.

BUBBLY OCEAN BIN

MESSINESS

5

PREP TIME

5 minutes

ACTIVITY TIME

20 minutes

MATERIALS

¼ cup water

2 tablespoons dish soap

Food processor or blender

Blue food coloring

Plastic bin

Plastic ocean animals

Container of water

PREP

Pour the water and dish soap into the food processor. Add a few drops of food coloring. Turn the food processor on for about a minute, or until the soap foam rises to the top. Scoop the soap foam into a plastic bin. Place the ocean animals inside.

STEPS

1. Watch as your toddler pretends the soap foam is the ocean and plays with the ocean animals.

2. Show your child how to rinse off the animals in the container of water.

COLOR DROP

MESSINESS

2

PREP TIME

30 minutes

ACTIVITY TIME

15 minutes

MATERIALS

20 **Q-tips**

Paintbrush

5 colors of paint: red, yellow, green, blue, and purple

Drill

Canister with a lid
(like a hot chocolate container)

PREP

Paint the ends of the Q-tips with the five colors of paint. While they are drying, drill five holes in the top of the canister. Outline the holes in paint with each color.

STEPS

1. Have your toddler match the colored Q-tips to the holes in the canister by sticking the Q-tips in the matching holes.

2. Let your toddler play until all the Q-tips are matched; repeat until your toddler tires of the game.

CAUTION *Keep your child away from the drill.*

find the Gold Coins

MESSINESS

1

PREP TIME

5 minutes

ACTIVITY TIME

15 minutes

MATERIALS

10 plastic gold coins

Permanent marker

Gold coins are symbolic for St. Patrick's Day. Legend says if you find the end of a rainbow, you'll see a leprechaun sitting on a pot of gold. This game challenges your toddler to find 10 gold coins.

PREP

Write the numbers 1 through 10 on the gold coins. Hide them around the room.

STEPS

1. Show your toddler what a gold coin looks like. Ask them to search the room for 10 gold coins.

2. Once they find the coins, count them to make sure they have all ten.

3. Older toddlers can practice lining up the coins in order from 1 to 10.

SHAVING CREAM SPLAT

MESSINESS

5

PREP TIME

5 minutes

ACTIVITY TIME

10 minutes

MATERIALS

Marker

Cotton pads

Plastic tablecloth

**Shaving cream or
whipped cream**

Toy hammer

PREP

Write the numbers 1 through 5 on the cotton pads.
Lay a plastic tablecloth down over a table or on the
floor. Squirt a dollop of shaving cream in various spots
around the tablecloth. Gently set a cotton pad on top
of each dollop.

STEPS

1. Say a number and have your toddler find that
   number on a cotton pad.

2. Ask your toddler to use a toy hammer to smash the
   cotton pad with that number. Watch as the shaving
   cream splats out!

CRUNCHY BIN

MESSINESS

3

PREP TIME

None

ACTIVITY TIME

15 minutes

MATERIALS

**Crunchy items such as
cereal, pretzels, puffs,
and dry noodles**

Plastic bin

Toy hammer

STEPS

1. Help your toddler pour crunchy items into a plastic
   bin. Pour enough to coat the bottom of the bin.

2. Let your toddler use a toy hammer to smash
   the food.

TIP *This is a good way to dispose of stale
items from your pantry.*

STUFF THE POM-POM

MESSINESS

2

PREP TIME

5 minutes

ACTIVITY TIME

15 minutes

MATERIALS

Scissors

**Empty canister
with a lid**
(like an oatmeal container)

Large pom-poms

Bowl

PREP

Cut a hole in the lid of the canister. Make the hole slightly smaller than the pom-pom. Set a bowl of pom-poms next to the canister.

STEPS

1. Say a color and ask your toddler to look for that colored pom-pom.

2. Have your toddler use their fingers to stuff the pom-pom into the canister.

3. Repeat these steps until all the pom-poms are inside.

4. Empty the container and start again.

CAUTION *Keep your child away from the scissors.*

FOAMY BATH PAINT

MESSINESS

4

PREP TIME

10 minutes

ACTIVITY TIME

20 minutes

MATERIALS

Shaving cream

Saline solution

Muffin tin

Spoon

Food coloring

Bathtub filled with water

Paintbrush

PREP

Add ¼ cup of shaving cream and 1 teaspoon of saline solution to each muffin tin compartment. Stir well. Mix 1 or 2 drops of food coloring into each compartment.

STEPS

1. Fill a bathtub with water and let your toddler use the paintbrush to create designs with the paint on the sides of the tub.

2. Ask your child about what they are painting.

COLOR SEARCH GAME

MESSINESS

3

PREP TIME

None

ACTIVITY TIME

20 minutes

MATERIALS

Construction paper

3 to 5 plastic bins

Items from around the house

STEPS

1. Place a piece of colored construction paper into each plastic bin.

2. Ask your toddler to look around the house to find one item that matches the color on each bin, and place it into the bin.

3. To make it more of a competition, let your toddler race with a sibling or see if they can find an item for every bin in under five minutes.

CATCH THE FISH

MESSINESS

4

PREP TIME

None

ACTIVITY TIME

20 minutes

MATERIALS

Large plastic bin

Water

Blue food coloring

Plastic toy fishes

Large slotted spoon

STEPS

1. Fill a large plastic bin with water and add a few drops of blue food coloring.

2. Have your toddler drop in the plastic fish. Let them use a large spoon to catch all the fish.

3. To make this activity more challenging, place other animals in the bin and see if your toddler can scoop up only the fish.

* SKILLS LEARNED *

ALPHABET MATCH

MESSINESS

2

PREP TIME

5 minutes

ACTIVITY TIME

15 minutes

MATERIALS

Marker

10 magnetic alphabet letters

10 sheets of construction paper

Magnetic surface
(like a cookie sheet or refrigerator)

Tape

Basket

PREP

Trace each alphabet magnet on 1 piece of construction paper. (The letters don't have to be in order.) Tape the paper to a magnetic surface. Place the ten alphabet magnets in a basket next to it.

STEPS

1. Ask your toddler to pick a letter from the basket and find its match on the piece of paper. You may have to help them put the letter right side up.

2. Have your child make matches until the basket is empty.

3. Repeat this activity with a new set of letters.

MATCHING COLORS

MESSINESS

2

PREP TIME

10 minutes

ACTIVITY TIME

15 minutes

MATERIALS

12 small craft sticks

Markers

Egg carton

Scissors

PREP

Color the bottom fourth of six craft sticks using a different color for each; then, color six more the same way with the same colors so that each craft stick has a match. Make a slit on the top of every compartment of an egg carton. Mix up the sticks and slide them into each slot in the egg carton with the colored end hidden in the carton.

STEPS

1. Ask your toddler to draw a stick, look at the color, and identify it.

2. Have your toddler pull out another stick and see if the colors match. If they find the match, they can keep the sticks. If they don't, they put both sticks back into their spots.

3. Take turns with your toddler until all the matches have been found.

CAUTION *Keep your child away from the scissors.*

BALANCING ACT GAME

MESSINESS

3

PREP TIME

None

ACTIVITY TIME

15 minutes

MATERIALS

Golf tees

Styrofoam block

Toy hammer

Lids from an empty applesauce or yogurt container

STEPS

1. Poke a golf tee into a block of Styrofoam and have your toddler hammer it in. Add golf tees all around the top of the block.

2. Ask your toddler to place a lid on top of each golf tee. See if your toddler can balance all the lids before they fall.

STICKER SORT

MESSINESS

2

PREP TIME

None

ACTIVITY TIME

15 minutes

MATERIALS

Painter's tape

Large stickers with themes such as happy and sad, stars and circles, red and blue, etc.

PREP

Tear off a piece of painter's tape and make a vertical line on the wall. On one side of the tape, place one sticker, such as a happy face. On the other side, place the opposite sticker, such as a sad face.

STEPS

1. Teach your toddler how to peel the backs off of stickers.

2. Ask your toddler to sort the stickers based on theme. Talk about the differences between the stickers.

3. Have your toddler place the stickers on either side of the tape, organized by theme.

BOOK DOMINOES

MESSINESS

2

PREP TIME

None

ACTIVITY TIME

10 minutes

MATERIALS

10 board books

STEPS

1. Set the board books upright and in a line. Leave about 5 inches between the books.

2. Once the books are in a line, have your toddler gently knock down the first book. The rest of the books should tumble over.

3. Try experimenting with creating a different setup, such as putting the books in a circle.

ROLL AND COUNT

MESSINESS

2

PREP TIME

None

ACTIVITY TIME

15 minutes

MATERIALS

Pair of dice

Cereal
(your toddler's favorite
variety, if possible)

Muffin tin

STEPS

1. Have your toddler roll the dice. Count the dots on the dice with your toddler. Ask your toddler to place that number of cereal pieces into a muffin tin compartment.

2. Repeat the game until each compartment is filled.

3. Eat the cereal when you're done!

TIP *Use large dice with children who put items in their mouths.*

ANIMAL MEMORY GAME

MESSINESS

1

PREP TIME

5 minutes

ACTIVITY TIME

15 minutes

MATERIALS

Animal stickers

10 paper plates

Markers

PREP

Place the same sticker or draw a picture of the same animal on 2 paper plates. Repeat until you have 5 pairs (10 plates). Mix them up and place them facedown on the floor.

STEPS

1. Have your toddler turn over two paper plates to see if they are a match. If they are, they can keep the paper plates. If not, your child should place them facedown in the same spot.

2. Take turns finding matches. Once all matches are found, count how many paper plates each player has. Whoever has the most is the winner.

SHAPE SEARCH

MESSINESS

3

PREP TIME

5 minutes

ACTIVITY TIME

20 minutes

MATERIALS

Large plastic bin

Rice

**Wooden blocks of
various shapes**

Large piece of paper

Marker

PREP

Fill a bin with rice. Trace the outline of all the blocks
onto a piece of paper. Bury the blocks in the rice.

STEPS

1. Ask your toddler to find a shape and match it to its
   outline on the paper.

2. Continue finding shapes until all of them have been
   matched up.

BABY ANIMAL GAME

MESSINESS

1

PREP TIME

None

ACTIVITY TIME

15 minutes

MATERIALS

None

STEPS

1. Have your toddler hide and make a baby animal noise.

2. Try finding your toddler by listening to their animal noise.

3. Trade places and have your toddler find you by listening to the animal sound.

CARD DROP

MESSINESS

3

PREP TIME

5 minutes

ACTIVITY TIME

15 minutes

MATERIALS

Shoebox

Utility knife

Deck of cards

PREP

Make a slit on the top of the shoebox that is large enough for a card to go through.

STEPS

1. Place a deck of cards by your toddler and ask them to stick the cards into the slot in the box.

2. They should continue sliding the cards in until all the cards are gone.

CAUTION *Keep your child away from the utility knife.*

NUMBERED CAR GAME

MESSINESS

1

PREP TIME

5 minutes

ACTIVITY TIME

15 minutes

MATERIALS

10 small toy cars

Masking tape

Marker

PREP

Place a small piece of masking tape on the top of each car. Use a marker to write the numbers 1 through 10 on the tape. Write the numbers 1 through 10 on other pieces of masking tape and place the numbered tape pieces around the room.

STEPS

1. Show your toddler the cars and practice identifying the numbers and counting them.

2. Have your toddler choose a car and drive it around the room looking for the matching piece of tape. Once they find it, they should park the car on it.

3. Repeat this until all the cars have been parked.

BUTTON SORT

MESSINESS

2

PREP TIME

5 minutes

ACTIVITY TIME

20 minutes

MATERIALS

Utility knife

Canister with a lid
(like an oatmeal or hot
chocolate container)

**3 permanent markers
that match the colors
of the buttons**

**Large colored buttons
in three colors**

Container

PREP

Make three slits in the canister. Make one slit in the top and two in the sides. Make sure the slits are large enough to pass a button through. Color the outline of the slits with a marker to match the button colors.

STEPS

1. Place a container of buttons next to the canister. Ask your toddler to choose a button and slip it into the matching slot.

2. Have your toddler continue sort the buttons until all of them are in the canister.

3. Have your child shake the container and listen to the loud sound it makes.

CAUTION *Keep your child away from the utility knife.*

DIGGING FOR BONES

MESSINESS

3

PREP TIME

30 minutes

ACTIVITY TIME

20 minutes

MATERIALS

Baking sheet

Aluminum foil

1 tablespoon instant yeast

Bowl

½ cup warm water

1 teaspoon honey

1 teaspoon salt

1⅓ cup flour

Beaten egg

Plastic bin

Cornmeal

PREP

Preheat the oven to 425°F. Line the baking sheet with aluminum foil. Pour the yeast into a bowl with the warm water, and stir until the yeast is dissolved. Add the honey and salt. Stir in the flour and then knead the mixture. If the mixture is sticky, add a little more flour. Roll pieces of the mixture to look like bones and put them on a baking sheet. Brush on the beaten egg and sprinkle a little salt on top. Bake for 10 minutes. While they are baking, fill a plastic bin with cornmeal. Once the bones have cooled, bury them under the cornmeal in the bin.

STEPS

1. Have your toddler find all the dinosaur bones.

2. Count how many bones you find and then enjoy them for a snack!

CAUTION *Keep your child away from the oven.*

SPIDERWEB BASKET

MESSINESS

3

PREP TIME

5 minutes

ACTIVITY TIME

15 minutes

MATERIALS

Small stuffed animals or toys

Laundry basket

String

PREP

Place stuffed animals and toys at the bottom of the laundry basket. Tie the end of the string to one side of the basket. Thread it through the basket in any pattern you desire until you create a web. Once it's finished, tie the end to the side.

STEPS

1. Ask your toddler to rescue the stuffed animals and toys from the spiderweb.

2. Have your child use their hands to reach through the web and pull the animals out.

GARBAGE DUMP

MESSINESS

4

PREP TIME

5 minutes

ACTIVITY TIME

15 minutes

MATERIALS

Masking tape

**1 package
of pom-poms**

Toy garbage truck

Plastic bin

PREP

Use tape to make a large rectangle on the floor for
the garbage dump. Place a bin of pom-poms and a toy
garbage truck on the other side of the room.

STEPS

1. Let your toddler fill up the garbage truck with
   pom-poms.

2. Have your child roll the truck across the floor to
   reach the dump and empty the pom-poms.

3. Have your toddler repeat this until all the pom-poms
   have been dumped.

4. To make this a competition, ask your toddler to
   race against a sibling, or time your toddler with
   a stopwatch.

DIG FOR SHELLS

MESSINESS

4

PREP TIME

5 minutes

ACTIVITY TIME

15 minutes

MATERIALS

Sand

Plastic bin

Water

Shells

Container of water

PREP

Pour the sand into a bin. Add water to make the sand slightly wet. Bury the shells in the sand. Place a container of water next to the bin.

STEPS

1. Ask your toddler to find all the shells and rinse them off in the water.

2. Have your toddler sort the shells by size.

ERASING GAME

MESSINESS

1

PREP TIME

None

ACTIVITY TIME

10 minutes

MATERIALS

Ice cube tray

Dry erase marker

**Small cloth for
an eraser**

STEPS

1. Turn an ice cube tray upside down.

2. Draw an alphabet letter with the dry erase marker
   on each compartment.

3. Say an alphabet letter. Let your toddler find it and
   erase it with a cloth.

4. Keep naming and finding letters until all of them
   have been erased.

   TIP *Try this activity using numbers
   or shapes.*

STICKY NOTES SORT

MESSINESS

2

PREP TIME

5 minutes

ACTIVITY TIME

15 minutes

MATERIALS

Masking tape

4 different colored pieces of paper

20 sticky notes, 5 in each of the 4 colors of paper

PREP

Tape the colored pieces of paper to the wall. Stick 20 sticky notes to the wall next to the papers, in random color order.

STEPS

1. Invite your toddler to find a sticky note and stick it to the matching colored paper.

2. See if your child can sort all the sticky notes in less than 5 minutes.

3. To make the activity harder, have your toddler sort 30 or more sticky notes.

FLY SWATTER COLOR GAME

MESSINESS
2

PREP TIME
None

ACTIVITY TIME
10 minutes

MATERIALS
Tape

Sheets of paper in different colors

Fly swatter
(clean)

STEPS

1. Tape colored paper to the wall.

2. Say a color and have your toddler slap the colored paper with a fly swatter.

3. Say 2 or 3 color names. See if your toddler can remember the order and slap the correct colored papers.

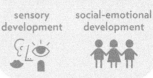
POND IN THE SINK

MESSINESS

3

PREP TIME

10 minutes

ACTIVITY TIME

15 minutes

MATERIALS

Sink

Blue food coloring

Green foam sheets

Scissors

Plastic toy frogs

Cups

PREP

Fill the sink with water. Add a few drops of blue food coloring. Cut foam sheets to look like lily pads and place them in the water. Set plastic animals on the lily pads or in the pond water.

STEPS

1. Have your toddler play with the pond sink. They can pretend the toy frogs are hopping on the lily pads.

2. Let your toddler scoop and pour the water with cups.

CAUTION *Keep your child away from the scissors.*

BUBBLE WRAP STOMP

MESSINESS

1

PREP TIME

None

ACTIVITY TIME

15 minutes

MATERIALS

Bubble wrap

Tape

STEPS

1. Have your toddler place one foot on a piece of bubble wrap. Use tape to wrap it around their foot. Repeat for the other foot.

2. Ask your toddler to walk around and listen to the popping noise their bubble-wrapped feet make.

3. Say an action and have them try it out: march, hop, stomp, or run around.

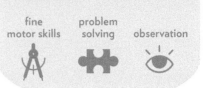

fine
motor skills

problem
solving

observation

· SKILLS LEARNED ·

BEAD MAZE

MESSINESS

2

PREP TIME

5 minutes

ACTIVITY TIME

15 minutes

MATERIALS

Pipe cleaners

Colander

**Wooden beads
with large holes**

Tape

PREP

Stick one end of a pipe cleaner into a hole of the colander. Bend it slightly and tape it to the inside of the colander so it doesn't move around. Thread large beads onto the pipe cleaner and then stick the other end through another hole. Bend the end and tape it down. Repeat to make more.

STEPS

1. Have your toddler use their fingers to move the beads around the colander.

2. If a bead gets stuck because another pipe cleaner is in the way, have your toddler problem solve to find a different way to move the bead.

3. Have your child count the beads on each pipe cleaner and see which one has the most.

TOSS THE BALL

MESSINESS

2

PREP TIME

None

ACTIVITY TIME

15 minutes

MATERIALS

4 laundry baskets

Marker

4 sheets of paper

Tape

Nerf balls

STEPS

1. Place four laundry baskets next to each other in a line.

2. Write the numbers 1 through 4 on individual sheets of paper and tape them to the sides of the laundry baskets in numerical order.

3. Ask your child to toss a ball into a particular basket, and see which numbered basket it lands in.

4. Sing this song while you toss the ball.

Tune: "The Farmer in the Dell"

I'm gonna make a throw.
Let's see how far this goes.
I toss it in the air and see
What basket will it be?

* SKILLS LEARNED *

COTTON BALL HOCKEY

MESSINESS

2

PREP TIME

None

ACTIVITY TIME

10 minutes

MATERIALS

Masking tape

Cotton balls

Straw

STEPS

1. Make a rectanglar box on the floor using tape. Call it a goal.

2. Place a pile of cotton balls and a straw a few feet away.

3. Ask your toddler to take one cotton ball and use the straw to blow it into the goal.

4. Time your child to see how many cotton balls they can get into the goal in 3 minutes.

MOVEMENT FREEZE SONG

MESSINESS

1

PREP TIME

None

ACTIVITY TIME

5 minutes

MATERIALS

None

STEPS

1. To release energy, sing and do the actions to this song:

MOVEMENT FREEZE SONG

Tune: "Do You Know the Muffin Man?"

Do you like to *jump* around?
Jump around, *jump* around?
Do you like to *jump* around?
Jump, and now let's *freeze*.
(freeze until you hear the next action)

Do you like to *crawl* around?
Crawl around, *crawl* around?
Do you like to *crawl* around?
Crawl, and now let's *freeze*.

Do you like to *hop* around?
Hop around, *hop* around?
Do you like to *hop* around?
Hop, and now let's *freeze*.

Do you like to *roll* around?
Roll around, *roll* around?
Do you like to *roll* around?
Roll, and now let's *freeze*.

Do you like to *run* around?
Run around, *run* around?
Do you like to *run* around?
Run, and now let's *freeze*.

Do you like to *tiptoe walk*?
Tiptoe walk, tiptoe walk?
Do you like to *tiptoe walk*?
Tiptoe, now let's *freeze*.

RING TOSS

MESSINESS

2

PREP TIME

5 minutes

ACTIVITY TIME

15 minutes

MATERIALS

Pencil

Paper towel tube

Paper bowl

Scissors

3 paper plates

PREP

Trace the end of a paper towel tube onto the bottom of the paper bowl. Cut around the circle in the bowl to create a hole. Place the paper towel tube into the hole. This will be your stake for the ring toss game. Cut the center out of three paper plates to create rings.

STEPS

1. Have your toddler toss the paper plate rings toward the stake with the goal of trying to land around it.

2. Place the stake farther away and see if your toddler can land the rings onto the stake.

   CAUTION *Keep your child away from the scissors.*

Egg Racing Game

MESSINESS

2

PREP TIME

5 minutes

ACTIVITY TIME

15 minutes

MATERIALS

20 or more plastic eggs

Plastic bins

Colorful eggs are fun to play with in the springtime. This racing game is sure to burn energy for your toddler, as well as practice sorting colors!

PREP

Place all the eggs in one bin. On the opposite side of the room, place the same number of bins as the number of colors of eggs. Place one colored egg into each bin so your toddler knows how to sort the eggs.

STEPS

1. Ask your toddler to choose a plastic egg, run to the other side of the room, and place the egg in the matching colored bin.

2. Have your toddler do this until all the eggs are sorted.

3. Count how many eggs are in each bin and see which color had the most.

4. To make it competitive, see if your toddler can sort the colored eggs in less than 5 minutes.

RACING ON THE 8

MESSINESS

2

PREP TIME

5 minutes

ACTIVITY TIME

15 minutes

MATERIALS

Masking tape
Toy cars

PREP

Make a large "8" with tape on the floor.

STEPS

1. Have your toddler race the toy cars on the number 8.

2. Sing this song while they play:

LET'S MAKE AN 8

Tune: "Down by the Bay"

Let's make an 8.
Oh, it's so great!
Let's make an 8.
Oh, it's so great!
Let's make an 8.
Oh, it's so great!
Have you seen how my cars,
race around the 8?
Let's make an 8!

GIANT HOURGLASS TIMER

MESSINESS

1

PREP TIME

5 minutes

ACTIVITY TIME

10 minutes

MATERIALS

Funnel

2 empty 2-liter bottles

2 cups rice

Tape

PREP

Place the funnel into a 2-liter bottle and pour the rice into it. Place another bottle on top so that it looks like an hourglass. Tape the open ends together.

STEPS

1. Help your child turn the hourglass upside down so the rice pours down. They should watch and listen to the sound it makes as the rice passes through the necks of the bottles.

2. When they tip the hourglass over, have your toddler clap, spin around, jump, make silly faces, and stomp their feet. See how many times they can do each action before time runs out.

3. When they're done playing with the giant hourglass, talk about which action your toddler enjoyed the most.

CONNECT THE BALLS

MESSINESS

2

PREP TIME

5 minutes

ACTIVITY TIME

15 minutes

MATERIALS

Circle-shaped Velcro pieces with sticky backs

20 ping-pong balls

PREP

Stick Velcro pieces onto two sides of each ping-pong ball, alternating the hook and loop sides.

STEPS

1. Show your toddler how to stick the balls together by matching the Velcro pieces.

2. Have your child stick the balls together to build a structure.

* SKILLS LEARNED *

ROLLING BALLS

MESSINESS

1

PREP TIME

5 minutes

ACTIVITY TIME

20 minutes

MATERIALS

Pool noodle

Serrated knife

Ping-pong balls

Golf balls

PREP

Cut a pool noodle in half lengthwise using the serrated knife. Set the pool noodle on the stairs or on a driveway outside.

STEPS

1. Have your toddler place a ping-pong ball at the top of the pool noodle. Ask them to let it go and watch the ball race down to the bottom.

2. Have your toddler try using a heavier ball such as a golf ball and find out which one was the fastest.

   TIP *To make cleanup easier, add a bucket to the bottom of the pool noodle to collect the balls.*

   CAUTION *Keep your child away from the serrated knife.*

POM-POM SHAKING GAME

MESSINESS

3

PREP TIME

5 minutes

ACTIVITY TIME

15 minutes

MATERIALS

Shoe box lid

Utility knife

Pom-poms

Wax paper

Masking tape

PREP

Cut 5 holes in the lid with the utility knife. Make sure the holes are about 2 inches wide, so a pom-pom can fit through it. Place a handful of pom-poms in the corner of the lid. Lay a piece of wax paper on top and tape the sides down so the pom-poms stay inside.

STEPS

1. Ask your toddler to move the lid around with the goal of shaking all the pom-poms out.

2. Let them try shaking, shifting, and tipping the lid to move the pom-poms around.

3. Make sure they keep moving the box until all the pom-poms have dropped out.

CAUTION *Keep your child away from the utility knife.*

RESOURCES

BOOKS

Zero to Two: The Book of Play by multiple authors
>This e-book has 25 simple play ideas for young toddlers. It also includes printable items, such as puppets for fingerplays.
>https://nurturestore.co.uk/zero-two-book-play-activities-for-babies-toddlers

Busy Bags Kids Will Love by Sara McClure
>This book contains 52 busy bag activities. Busy bags are make-ahead kits for children to play with during quiet times. The ideas are simple to set up and encourage learning.

The Basics of Fine Motor Skills by Heather Greutman
>Heather clearly explains fine motor development with simple explanations and descriptions. She also shares many fine motor activities, which are broken down by category and age.

A Year of Educational Quiet Bins: The Secret to Peaceful Days with Kids by Sarah Noftle
>This book contains 52 quiet bin ideas to help calm the chaos in your day. These ideas are simple to set up and can be used all throughout the year.

Learn with Play: 150+ Activities for Year-Round Fun & Learning by multiple authors (including myself)
>A collection of kid activity bloggers worked together to put their best play ideas into one book. This contains activities for play, crafts, early learning, life skills, and seasonal activities.

99 Fine Motor Ideas for ages 1 to 5 by multiple authors
This book offers 99 ideas for fine motor development. The activities include toys, busy bags, sensory play, life skills, arts and crafts, and seasonal activities.
https://www.amazon.com/99-Fine-Motor-Ideas-Ages/dp/1500956791

The Importance of Play in Promoting Healthy Child Development and Maintaining Strong Parent-Child Bonds by Kenneth R. Ginsburg
This article highlights the benefits to play and how it is vital to a child's healthy development. It shares the research done on reduced child-driven play and factors that have changed the routine of childhood. In the end, the article shares ideas on how pediatricians can promote the importance of play for families, school systems, and communities.
http://pediatrics.aappublications.org/content/119/1/182

WEBSITES

Hands On as We Grow https://www.handsonaswegrow.com
Jamie Reimer shares wonderful ways to play with your children. All her ideas use simple materials that promote learning for toddlers and preschoolers.

Growing Hands-On Kids https://www.growinghandsonkids.com
Heather Greutman is an occupational therapy assistant and she shares helpful tips for child development, occupational therapy tips, behavior and sensory processing information, and hands-on activities.

Teaching 2 and 3 Year Olds https://teaching2and3yearolds.com
Sheryl Cooper is a teacher in a toddler classroom. She shares many wonderful ideas and tips for teachers and parents, which includes hands-on learning activities, sensory play, book lists, and printables.

Fun Learning for Kids https://funlearningforkids.com
Danielle Buckley has amazing play ideas for your children on her blog. She also has beautiful free printables and fun games for little ones.

REFERENCES

The Importance of Play in Promoting Healthy Child Development and Maintaining Strong Parent-Child Bond: Focus on Children in Poverty
   http://pediatrics.aappublications.org/content/129/1/e204.full

Child Development and Early Learning
   http://www.factsforlifeglobal.org/03/1.html

INDEX

ACKNOWLEDGMENTS

There are so many people who have helped make my dream of writing this book a reality. At the top of the list is Callisto Media. They have been a helpful source of encouragement and problem solving during this book-writing process. A big thanks to them for taking a leap of faith with asking me to write this book.

Thank you to my husband, Lane, who is my ultimate rock. You are always my listening ear, my source of encouragement, and my biggest supporter. Thank you for showing me love every single day.

I am so thankful for my three beautiful boys: Troy, Wesley, and Lincoln. They are the inspiration behind all my activities. Thank you for being my guinea pigs and for being so excited to try out my ideas. I am so blessed to be your mom!

Thank you to my incredible parents and in-laws: Brad and Kristi Smith and William and Kathryn Thayer. Your love and support are with me in whatever I pursue. Thank you for watching our children so I had time to write this book.

I am so grateful for my amazing blogging friends, who are always supporting me and inspiring me. Above all, thank you to my group of cheerleaders who keep me accountable. Sharla, Heather, and Bethany—I couldn't have done it without you!

Thank you to all the loyal Teaching Mama readers for your encouragement and support!

Most importantly, thank you to God, who has given me the strength, wisdom, and courage to pursue my dreams. I am forever grateful for the experiences He has brought into my life.

ABOUT THE AUTHOR

ANGELA THAYER was a classroom teacher before deciding to stay home full-time with her three boys. Her passion for educating children and making learning fun led her to create the website TeachingMama.org. Her mission is to provide parents and teachers with the tools they need to create a rich early childhood experience for children. She currently lives in Iowa with her husband and children.